COMPENDIUM FOR
THE CIVIC ECONOMY

a **00:/** production

Published by:

00:/
81 Leonard street
EC2A 4QS
London

+44 (0)20 7739 2230

info@research00.net
www.research00.net

In association with NESTA & Design Council CABE

ISBN 978-0-9568210-0-3

For more information about this book, please visit:

www.civiceconomy.net (hosted by 00:/)
or contact:
hello@civiceconomy.net

MIX
Paper from
responsible sources
FSC® C007915

First edition May 2011
Printed and bound by Calverts Co-operative
Printed on FSC Recycled Paper Revive 100 Uncoated Paper

Typeface design:
Body typeface: Caecilia LT Std
Title typeface: AW Conqueror Inline
Other: Myriad Pro

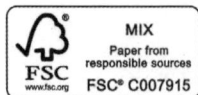

CONTENTS

03   Preface by NESTA and Design Council CABE

05   Foreword by the Prime Minister

Introduction

08-13   Introducing the civic economy

Case Studies

16-21	#01	Arcola Theatre			
22-27	#02	Baisikeli			
28-33	#03	Brixton Village			
34-39	#04	Bromley by Bow Centre			
40-45	#05	Brooklyn Superhero Supply Co.			
46-51	#06	Fab Lab Manchester			
52-57	#07	Fintry Development Trust			
58-63	#08	The George and Dragon			
64-69	#09	Household Energy Services			
70-75	#10	The Hub Islington			
76-81	#11	Hørsholm Waste-to-Energy			
82-87	#12	Incredible Edible Todmorden			
88-93	#13	Jayride			
94-99	#14	Livity			
100-105	#15	Museum of East Anglian Life			
106-111	#16	Neil Sutherland Architects			
112-117	#17	Nottingham University Hospitals			
118-123	#18	Olinda Psychiatric Hospital			
124-129	#19	One Love City			
130-135	#20	The People's Supermarket			
136-141	#21	Rutland Telecom			
142-147	#22	Southwark Circle			
148-153	#23	Studio Hergebruik			
154-159	#24	TCHO			
160-165	#25	Tübingen User-led Housing			

Conclusion

168-171		Lessons learned
172-173	A	Recognising the protagonists
174-175	B	Participation beyond consultation
176-177	C	Financial co-investment
178-179	D	Re-using existing assets
180-181	E	The experience of place
182-183	F	An open-ended approach
184-185	G	Generating change through networks
186-187	H	Recognising where value lies
189		Building a civic economy future

192-193	Photographs
194	The 00:/ project team
195	Acknowledgements

A CIVIC ECONOMY IS EMERGING,
ONE WHICH IS FUNDAMENTALLY
BOTH OPEN AND SOCIAL.
IT'S AN ECONOMY WHICH IS
FUSING THE CULTURE OF WEB 2.0
WITH CIVIC PURPOSE.

Publication Partners

NESTA

...is the UK's foremost independent expert on how innovation can solve some of the country's major economic and social challenges. Our work is enabled by an endowment, funded by the National Lottery, and we operate at no cost to the government or taxpayer.

CABE

...as CABE and the Design Council come together, we're well placed to give a strong voice to architecture and design. Uniting two world-class centres of design excellence, our merger reflects the widening role and influence of design. Together, as a leaner, more focused 'enterprising charity' incorporated by Royal Charter, we're determined to put design at the heart of Britain's social and economic renewal. We receive grants from BIS and DCLG, and also receive funding from a variety of other sources.

00:/

...is a London based strategy & design practice. We are driven by an aspiration to create genuinely sustainable places founded on evidenced social, economic, and environmental principles. Our work focuses both on physical architecture and on the emergent institutions that can underpin and animate a successful built environment for the 21st Century, whether at the scale of a workspace, a neighbourhood or a city region.

1 Plough Place
London
EC4A 1DE

research@nesta.org.uk
www.nesta.org.uk

34 Bow Street
London
WC2E 7DL

cabe@designcouncil.org.uk
www.designcouncil.org.uk

81 Leonard Street
London
EC2A 4QS

info@research00.net
www.research00.net

PREFACE BY NESTA AND DESIGN COUNCIL CABE

We are in the midst of a difficult period of transition. In the wake of the global financial crisis, and as we become more acutely aware of the scarcity of environmental resources and the rising pressures of complex social issues, we need to find a more sustainable way to organise and grow our economy.

We commissioned this book because we knew there would be a lot to learn from the myriad of innovations that are already showing us how. The examples presented here are characteristic of what we call the 'civic economy' – combining the spirit of entrepreneurship with the aspiration of civic renewal. This is already a vibrant movement, with new ventures; networks and behaviours changing the appearance and economies of places across the UK.

From local food growing projects to sustainable supermarkets, community waste-to-energy plants to co-operative telecoms services, these initiatives are having a tangible impact on social interactions and economic opportunities in cities, villages and towns. They are even influencing the physical shape and appearance of these places, changing the way they are designed, built and used.

But in order to strengthen and grow a new civic economy, we need to know how it works. This is even more critical now as the Government extols the virtues of the Big Society and the potential for more locally-led innovation to address social issues. This book holds lessons for government, business, local authorities and communities in how to help these sorts of enterprises to grow and spread.

This book is an important and timely contribution to the debate which both NESTA and CABE – with its new home at the Design Council – are taking forward.

We welcome your comments and views.

FOREWORD BY
THE PRIME MINISTER

The idea at the heart of the Big Society is a very simple one: that real change can't come from government alone. We're only going to make life better for everyone in this country if everyone plays their part – if change in our economy and our society is driven from the bottom up.

Some people have been dismissive about this. They have claimed that there's no appetite for this change and that it's all too impractical. The great thing about this book is that it shows the type of entrepreneurship that generates civic action and the Big Society, and what it can achieve.

It demonstrates that there is public appetite for more civic action. The examples in these pages show people's real yearning to make a difference and feel more connected to their neighbourhoods. Whether it's the residents of Todmorden coming together to plant fruit trees or the crowds that flock to Brixton Market, it's clear that when the opportunity is there to volunteer or to support local enterprises, people grab it.

And this book blows apart the myth that civic action is impractical; something that might make people feel good but doesn't make a difference. The inspiring examples in these pages have achieved everything from supporting local farmers to reducing carbon emissions to helping educate children from disadvantaged backgrounds. These are real, tangible benefits – and they show just what a powerful difference can be made when people come together to make life better.

I welcome this book and congratulate all the social pioneers in its pages who have done their bit to improve the places we live in and the lives we lead. Keep up the good work.

David Cameron

The Rt Hon David Cameron MP

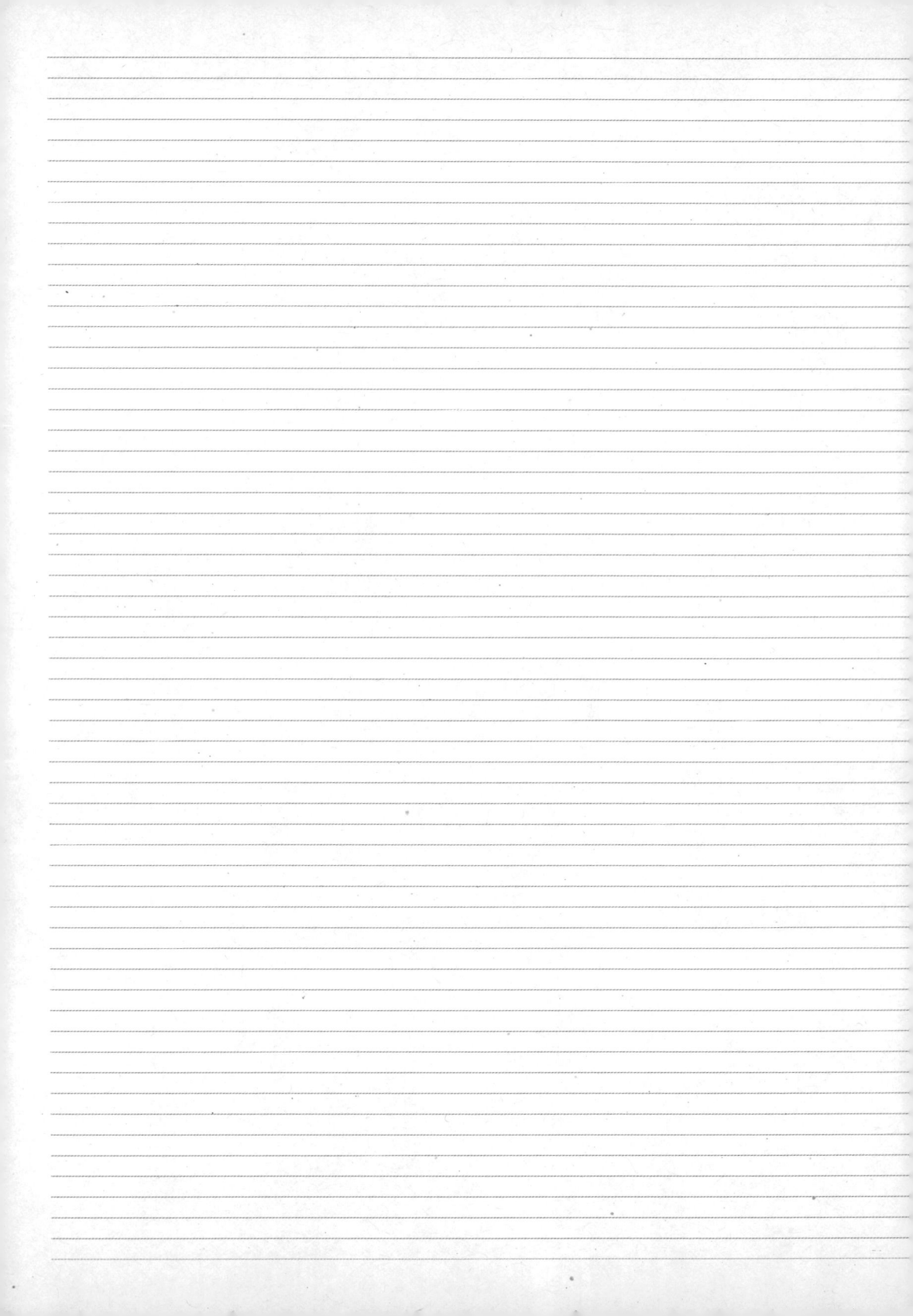

INTRODUCTION

1 - We are indebted to the work of Robin Murray, and his wider than usual
definition of the social economy is akin to what we call the civic economy. The
central point here is that the civic economy is not the exclusive domain of any
particular sector of the economy; instead, it bridges across the public, private
and organised third sector as well as including the public at large; Murray, R.
(2009) 'Danger and Opportunity – Crisis and the New Social Economy.' London:
Young Foundation & NESTA.

INTRODUCING
THE CIVIC ECONOMY

A new way of doing is starting to change places, communities and enterprise across Britain and beyond. In the aftermath of the financial crisis and against the context of deep environmental and social change, a collective reflection is taking place on how to build more sustainable routes to shared prosperity. But in the meantime, an increasing number and great diversity of change-makers are already getting on with the job of re-making local economies and places. Though locally driven, their initiatives are deeply rooted in global social, cultural and technological trends that originated well before the recent economic shocks.

As the political debate continues about the role and potential of the Big Society and StartUp Britain, this book brings together a wide range of inspiring examples that begin to illustrate what places built upon a different economy might look like: edible public spaces, crowd-funded workspaces for social entrepreneurs, peer-to-peer car sharing websites, and town centre markets revitalised by a fresh approach to igniting good ideas. The list is growing – and its potential is huge. This is a trend that goes beyond traditional divides between the public, private and third sectors; an attitude that questions all aspects of supply chains and makes them more equitable; an approach that enables citizens to be co-producers and investors instead of just consumers; and an opportunity to unlock and share the resources we have more effectively. This is the civic economy.

We define the civic economy as comprising people, ventures and behaviours that fuse innovative ways of doing from the traditionally distinct spheres of civil society, the market and the state. Founded upon social values and goals, and using deeply collaborative approaches to development, production, knowledge sharing and financing, the civic economy generates goods, services and common infrastructures in ways that neither the state nor the market economy alone have been able to accomplish. [1]

With this book we aim to achieve three things:

• Show that the civic economy is already a real, vital and growing part of our places, which actively contributes to community resilience, everyday innovation and shared prosperity.

• Outline in practical terms how different leaders in localities – that is, all those working together to improve places and their economies, whether in the public, private or third sector – can create the fertile ground for the civic economy to flourish and grow.

• Demonstrate that the potential of the civic economy to regenerate places and improve people's lives means that localities need to get better at recognising the role of diverse civic entrepreneurs and at understanding what enables them to create change in a wide range of contexts.

2 - Of the many authors one could connect with this, we would highlight (with regards to the broader economic and cultural shifts): Murray, R., Caulier-Grice, J. and Mulgan, G. (2009) 'Social Venturing.' London: NESTA; Leadbeater, C. (2008) 'We-Think.' London: Profile Books; Shirkey. C (2008) 'Here Comes Everybody: The Power of Organizing Without Organizations.' London: Penguin Books; Tapscott, D. and & Williams, A.D (2006). 'Wikinomics: How Mass Collaboration Changes Everything.' London: Portfolio; and (with regards to policy-making) Goldsmith, S. (2010) 'The Power of Social Innovation.' San Francisco: Jossey Bass; RSA (2010) 'From Social Security to Social Productivity: A Vision for 2020 Public Services – The final report of the Commission on 2020 Public Services.' London: Royal Society for the Arts, Commerce and Manufacturing; and (with regards to place-making) Markusen, A. and Gadwa, A. (2010) 'Creative Placemaking.' Washington: National Endowment for the Arts; Barrie, D. 'Open Source Place-Making: A Collective Approach to the Development of Cities in an Age of 'Big Society', Digital Media and Social Enterprise.' (http://www.scribd.com/doc/41008414/Open-Source-Place-making).

3 - See for example the Local Growth White Paper: HM Government (2010) 'Local Growth: Realising Every Place's Potential.' London: The Stationery Office. For a wider argument see for example, Sen, A. (1999) 'Development as Freedom.' Oxford, Oxford University Press.

The civic economy and its role today

The civic economy has been part of the UK's economic landscape for a long time – from the Co-operative Movement to the Mutual and Friendly Societies, and from the Mechanics' Institutes to housing associations. In the 19th century, it was a powerful force for good during the rapid changes of the Industrial Revolution, creating independent institutions and coalitions that improved people's lives and made places more resilient.

More than a century later, the civic economy is yet again in focus. Since the 1990s at least, the outlines of a profound economic and cultural shift have been visible, and chronicled by a wide range of observers. [2]

There are two fundamental drivers of this shift: firstly, a growing recognition that we need a different economic development model that enables genuine progress in addressing shared economic, social and environmental challenges; and, secondly, a fundamental transformation in how people and organisations can communicate and collaborate.

Hence we see an increasing overlap between traditionally distinct domains in the economy:

• A reforming state and public services, where the co-production of public goods and services between users and providers is becoming an established principle.

• An increasing number of values-driven private sector companies moving beyond traditional corporate social responsibility (CSR) to put social opportunities and ecological concerns at the core of operations, alongside a proliferation of hybrid business models that build on and bend traditional ownership structures.

• An increasing recognition that innovative working practices in and between organisations – based on the use of new social network technologies, collaboration tools and creative approaches to self-organisation, and tapping into both global and local connections – can create better outcomes.

• A widespread trend amongst the public at large to be directly involved in the (co-)creation of cultural and other products either in digital or physical spaces – through the established third sector or, just as often, in new ad-hoc groups or networks.

The global financial crisis and its aftermath put the civic economy and its potential further in the spotlight, as deep vulnerabilities in the UK's economic model as well in the social fabric of its places were exposed. This crisis prompts us to think anew about how to create a more balanced economy that generates sustainable prosperity and life chances for all. [3] Equally, the impact of the recession on public finances has prompted deeper questions about how public services can be sustained and improved in the face of public spending constraints.

4 - Conisbee, M et al. (2005) 'Clone Town Britain: The Loss of Local Identity on the Nation's High Streets.' London: New Economics Foundation; Dermot Finch: 'Time for a new Urban Task Force' (HYPERLINK "http://centreforcities.typepad.com/centre_for_cities/2010/03/time-for-a-new-urban-task-force.html"http://centreforcities.typepad.com/centre_for_cities/2010/03/time-for-a-new-urban-task-force.html); and the members of the 1999 commission that originated the very term 'urban renaissance' gave a critique on urban regeneration practice spurred by their original work in Urban Task Force (2005) 'Towards a Strong Urban Renaissance.' London: Urban Task Force.

5 - 00:/ has been involved with two of these projects: The Hub Islington (case study 10) and the Bristol Urban Beach (mentioned as an 'other example' under One Love City, case study 19).

The civic economy and places in the UK

The civic economy has the potential to transform how places are shaped. This is particularly important now that much of the regeneration and place-shaping practices of the past decade or so – often referred to as the 'urban renaissance' – have run out of steam. Not only has the property boom fizzled out, but more fundamental doubts have been raised about some of the key tenets of that urban renaissance. Whilst few would question in principle the benefits of a better public realm, investment in better-quality public buildings and higher design standards for homes and workplaces, in practice many problems remain unsolved.

Not all regeneration projects have genuinely looked beyond bricks and mortar; many localities rely heavily on public sector expenditure; town centres are overly dependent on the consuming (and debt-laden) public; the public are sceptical about their ability to actually influence area change; and risk-averse, routine-driven approaches to regeneration have resulted in a creeping homogenisation of places. As the New Economics Foundation aptly summarised, those places left behind by the boom have become ghost towns; but at the same time large-scale new developments and the gradual erosion of local character have all too often created 'clone towns'. [4]

As the impact of the recession and its aftermath continues to affect places across the UK, choices need to be made about how localities can best support a genuine recovery, particularly in the context of scarce resources. The growing civic economy is integral to this – which is why developers, landowners, architects, local authorities and all others collaborating to improve places should pay attention and learn from the examples presented in this book.

The task at hand: civic entrepreneurs and fertile ground

We argue that all those working to improve localities across the UK can be, and need to be, civic entrepreneurs. All of us need to play an active role in facilitating the emergence of the type of ventures presented here, whether they originate from within or outside established organisations. In practice, this means that those in leadership positions in policy-making, planning and finance need to relate actively to the emerging civic economy, and recognise their respective roles in enabling it to develop, connect and flourish. We call this 'fertile ground': creating the conditions for this new economy to grow.

Therefore, we urge all those working to improve places – whether as individuals or neighbourhood groups, as local authorities or developers, as business owners or as investors – to reflect on how the examples in this book could be relevant in local areas – and to recognise the wealth and potential of what is already going on.

This book: a reading guide

This book makes visible the potential of this civic economy to affect the places, economies and human interactions of our everyday lives: what this civic economy looks like in all its diversity, how these initiatives can grow, and what makes them possible. It shows the wide range of protagonists driving new ventures, analyses their different characteristics and draws out lessons of how to strengthen this potential.

We present 25 case studies – the story of their development, and the lessons they contain for planning and policy. [5]

We distil some critical ingredients to show how each venture has been made to work, which can serve as inspiration for others. Moreover, the case studies are not just stand-alone examples; we also draw together similar stories that share this success. In a concluding chapter, we show how different actors in localities can create the fertile ground we need to grow the civic economy through a range of practical recommendations.

CASE STUDIES

A lesson in renewable energy technologies at the Arcola Theatre

01

ARCOLA THEATRE

AN OPEN HOUSE FOR NEW IDEAS
LONDON, UNITED KINGDOM

'I was so excited when I found the Arcola, and discovered they were looking for volunteers. I had just moved to Hackney, and I really wanted to get involved in the local community – to make the Big Smoke feel a little smaller! So volunteering there was a great way of meeting friendly locals and getting to see some amazing free theatre. It's a real hidden gem, well-loved by locals and a favourite amongst the acting community too – I served a drink to Alan Rickman once!'

Anna Levy, former volunteer at Arcola

60%
AUDIENCE FROM LOCAL BOROUGHS OF HACKNEY & ISLINGTON

1,000
VOLUNTEERS HELPED ARCOLA THEATRE MOVE TO ITS NEW SITE

38%
REDUCTION IN CARBON FOOTPRINT PER EMPLOYEE IN 2009

EMBEDDING A THEATRE IN THE NEIGHBOURHOOD

2000   **2003**   **2007**   **2008**   **2011**

- THE ARCOLA THEATRE IS FOUNDED IN A FORMER FACTORY
- THE UK'S FIRST BLACK DRAMA SCHOOL IS SET UP IN ARCOLA
- ARCOLA ENERGY IS ESTABLISHED
- THE ARCOLA ISTANBUL IS SET UP IN AN OLD CAR FACTORY
- FIRST ARCOLA PRODUCTION USING LED LIGHT AND HYDROGEN FUEL CELLS
- THE ARCOLA LOSES ITS PREMISES AND MOVES TO ASHWIN STREET

ARCOLA ENERGY

VOLUNTEERS FROM A BANK HELP TO BUILD NEW WALLS

TURKISH-LANGUAGE PRODUCTION POWERED SOLELY BY RENEWABLES

ECO-CAFE WHERE VOLUNTEERS AND LOCALS HANG OUT

SUSTAINABILITY FOR SCHOOLS WORKSHOP

HALF-TERM CHILDREN'S OUTDOOR ACTIVITIES AT THE DALSTON GARDENS CO-CREATED BY ARCOLA

arcola theatre

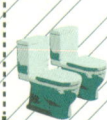

GREEN SUNDAY

- ARCOLA CAPOEIRA STREET DANCE WORKSHOP FOR LOCAL SCHOOLS
- SMART METERS SHOW ENERGY USAGE AND COST SAVINGS
- GREEN SUNDAY DEBATE WITH NEW ECONOMICS FOUNDATION AND FILM VIEWING
- YOUTH GROUP BRAINSTORMING CREATIVE POLICY IN THE BLOOMBERG ARTS LAB
- SUSTAINABLE ENERGY TECHNOLOGY INCUBATOR & SHOP
- TOILETS MADE WITH RECYCLED LOOS AND SINKS
- YOUNG PEOPLE GET TRAINING IN TECHNICAL AND EVENT PLANNING SKILLS AS PART OF ARCOLA'S CREATIVE INDUSTRIES NETWORK

THE STORY

Acting and environmental engineering might seem an odd mix. But for the Arcola Theatre in Dalston, it has proven a successful recipe for up-skilling young people, working with migrant groups, creating a resilient community asset and increasing eco-awareness in a highly diverse part of the London Borough of Hackney.

When the Arcola Theatre opened in a former textile factory in 2000, its founders, Turkish migrants Mehmet Ergen and Leyla Nazli, were determined to make it a place that was open for local initiatives. Realising the tremendous diversity of the area – over 100 languages are spoken in the vicinity of the Arcola Theatre – their ethos was to combine a welcoming attitude to community-driven projects with theatrical innovation and experimentation. The theatre was soon hosting a variety of productions set up by local groups, including young people, older residents, refugees and a host of ethnic and religious minority groups. As a consequence, 60% of its audiences are from the local boroughs of Hackney and Islington.

Arcola was created on a shoestring – the founders primarily used their own credit cards and personal savings – and the theatre has continued to run on minimal funds even as productions have scaled up. Every Tuesday it offers a number of 'pay what you can' tickets, as a way of making theatre more accessible to the local residents. To enable this approach, the Arcola has cultivated a network of volunteers, more than a hundred of whom regularly contribute their time and energy in a wide variety of capacities.

In 2005 one of them made a bold suggestion. Ben Todd, an engineer, suggested that the Arcola could add environmental sustainability to its social agenda and become the first carbon-neutral theatre in the UK. In accordance with the organisation's ethos, Nazli and Ergen gave Todd free rein to use the theatre as testing ground and demonstration platform. The result was Arcola Energy, which drives sustainability within the arts by providing advice and inspiration to other theatres, as well as becoming a commercial provider of sustainable energy solutions. In 2008, the theatre featured its first production powered by hydrogen fuel cells and lit by LED lamps, cutting its standard energy consumption by 60%.

Thus the organisation now consists of three mutually interdependent parts: the theatre, the charity that runs community and training programmes, and the energy company – with strong linkages that enable learning and co-development. Diversification into these different funding streams has also increased Arcola's resilience in the long term; although the theatre over time has obtained funding from organisations like the Arts Council, no single source makes up more than 15% of its revenue.

Its collaborative and innovative attitude has had other benefits: the Arcola has for example built strong relationships with Hackney Council, which has recognised the theatre's role in driving local sustainability initiatives. When, in 2010, the former factory was to be turned into luxury flats, the council took a proactive role in brokering a deal to find the theatre a new home.

In 2011, the new Arcola Theatre opened up in the Colourworks Factory, less than half a mile from its original site. The move took only a couple of months and was carried out with the help of more than 1,000 volunteers. Having moved to a larger site, the Arcola is now able to grow, offering bigger theatre productions as well as increasing its portfolio of partnerships and projects. It has already set up a sustainable energy incubator that will include elements of R&D as well as genuine small-scale manufacturing.

IMPACT

Beyond becoming a substantial cultural institution with a plethora of diverse and often high-end productions to its name and a hefty portfolio of community and social programmes, the Arcola has become a host and facilitator for a diverse array of local projects and enterprises. These range from a nearby community garden and the UK's first black drama school to an online energy store and the Greening Theatres initiative. In 2008 it set up a sister theatre in a former car factory in Istanbul, Turkey.

KEY LESSONS

RECOGNISING THE PROTAGONISTS

THE EXPERIENCE OF PLACE

AN OPEN-ENDED APPROACH

Space for local ideas

From the beginning, the Arcola Theatre has had a distinct ethos of allowing anyone with a good idea to try to kick-start their project within the space. The theatre both takes a hands-off approach, allowing budding entrepreneurs to experiment and lead projects themselves, as well as giving hands-on support for groups and individuals to implement their ideas. For instance, instead of being 'directed' by a programme leader, the Arcola Youth Theatre group is encouraged to write its own artistic policy and set up its own productions.

Making sustainability tangible

The Arcola had an opportunity to test the full reach of its sustainability agenda when it moved to its new location. The refurbishment of the building was an ideal pilot for pushing innovation as well as for expressing the organisation's ethos, for example, by using only a limited amount of new material resources. With the help of a wide range of volunteers and experts, existing materials were re-used, including walls, doors and scrap metal. Even the toilets and sinks were recycled. Making both the 'do it yourself' approach and the energy savings (e.g. through smart meters) evident in the very fabric of the place is crucial to conveying the values of the organisation and its ambition not just to be a sustainable theatre but also, through Arcola Energy, to drive change across the cultural sector.

A community-focused hybrid venture

From the start, the Arcola founders have taken an enterprising approach to the idea of a theatre as a local institution. By rethinking the theatre building as not only a space for cultural production but also a platform open to engaging in a wider range of innovative projects, and by mixing income streams, they have created a space that is not only socially and environmentally sustainable but also financially sustainable. Arcola has also showed openness to hybridising even further, responding to local people's suggestions and projects, thereby creating a truly inclusive and participative space.

IN CONCLUSION

How can local cultural institutions reach outside the walls of their premises and constraints of their traditional functions? By inclusive programming and outreach, and also by inviting entrepreneurial outsiders to be part of an open-ended approach. This may see these institutions become hybrid organisations based on the ideas, energy and drive of local people and local opportunities.

OTHER EXAMPLES

The Watershed, Bristol, UK, 1982
...is an arts venue and platform that has focused on improving the night-time culture of the city's harbour front; in the iShed it has created an incubator to enable and support innovation and collaboration between computing, communications and the creative industries.

junk4funk, Nottingham, UK, 2007
...is a company that produces recycled music instruments from everyday household waste, and offers music and sustainability workshops for schools, festivals and council events.

FARO (Fábrica de Artes y Oficios) de Oriente, Mexico City, Mexico, 2000
... is a cultural centre in one of the city's poorest and most violent areas; it engages local people in co-organising the security around local events, reducing the need for police involvement and creating a gang-free zone.

Baisikeli founders Henrik Mortensen and Niels Bonefeld sort dumped bicycles

02

BAISIKELI

AN ETHICAL BIKE SALVAGE SHOP
COPENHAGEN, DENMARK

'Baisikeli helps increase the mobility of both the Danish IKEA's co-workers and its customers, as well as African farmers, while also freeing the streets from dumped bikes and reducing CO_2 emissions. What's not to like?'

Jonas Engberg, IKEA Division of Sustainability

400,000
BICYCLES DUMPED IN
DENMARK EVERY YEAR

2,200
BICYCLES SENT TO
AFRICA SINCE 2007

£0
CHARITABLE
FUNDING

BUILDING A SELF-SUSTAINING VENTURE TO CREATE WEALTH FROM WASTE

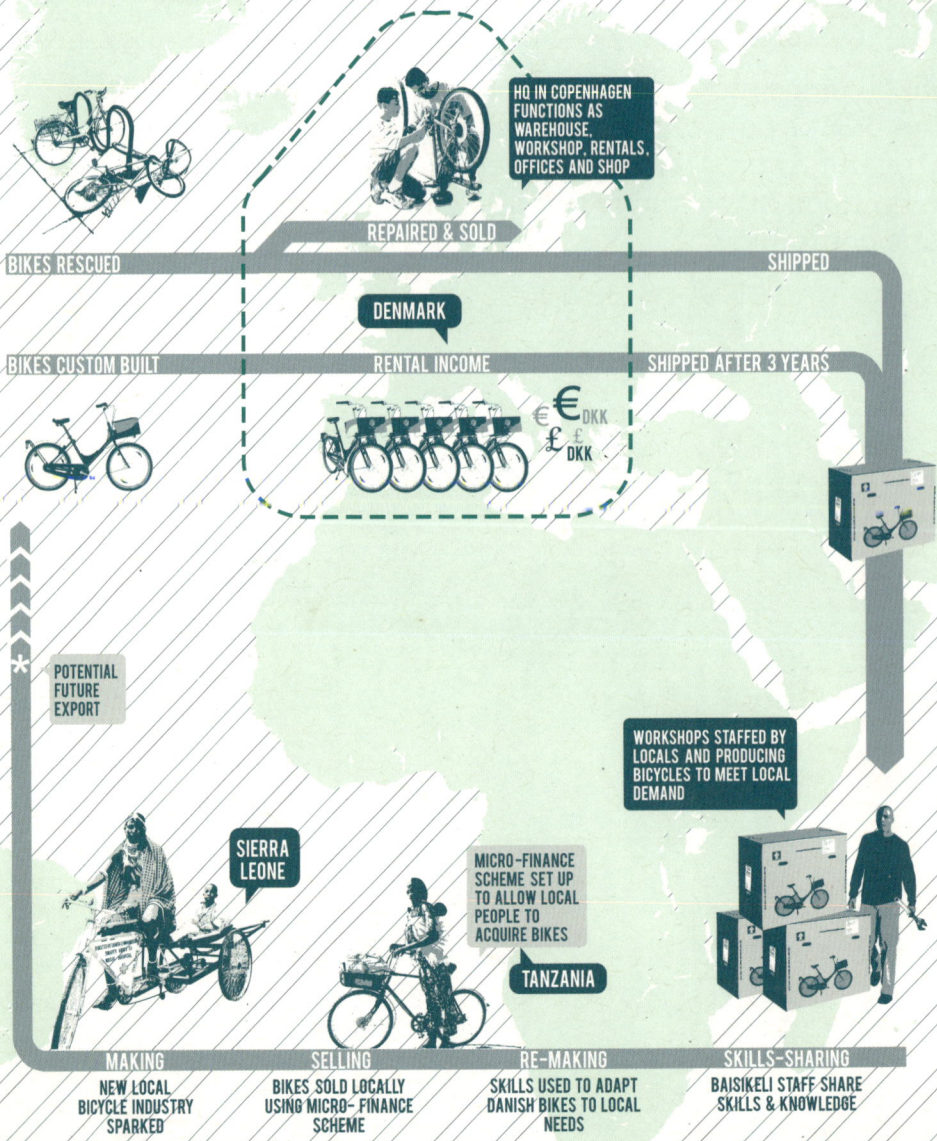

HQ IN COPENHAGEN FUNCTIONS AS WAREHOUSE, WORKSHOP, RENTALS, OFFICES AND SHOP

REPAIRED & SOLD

BIKES RESCUED

SHIPPED

DENMARK

BIKES CUSTOM BUILT

RENTAL INCOME

SHIPPED AFTER 3 YEARS

€ DKK
£ DKK

POTENTIAL FUTURE EXPORT

WORKSHOPS STAFFED BY LOCALS AND PRODUCING BICYCLES TO MEET LOCAL DEMAND

SIERRA LEONE

MICRO-FINANCE SCHEME SET UP TO ALLOW LOCAL PEOPLE TO ACQUIRE BIKES

TANZANIA

MAKING	SELLING	RE-MAKING	SKILLS-SHARING
NEW LOCAL BICYCLE INDUSTRY SPARKED	BIKES SOLD LOCALLY USING MICRO- FINANCE SCHEME	SKILLS USED TO ADAPT DANISH BIKES TO LOCAL NEEDS	BAISIKELI STAFF SHARE SKILLS & KNOWLEDGE

THE STORY

In the heart of Copenhagen's shopping district is one very different venture: Baisikeli is a bicycle salvage workshop, an ethical bike rental company and a remarkable international development initiative based on resource sharing, skills transfer and micro-loans.

Baisikeli started in 2003, when cousins Niels Bonefeld and Henrik Mortensen decided to connect Tanzania's urgent need for cheap transport with Denmark's growing mountain of discarded bikes. The idea was simple: Baisikeli would collect some of the 400,000 bicycles scrapped in Denmark every year and send them to Tanzania, where they would be repaired and sold at local market prices.

Although bureaucratic hurdles blocked the cousins' initial plan to collect bicycles from police lost property offices, they discovered that insurance companies were happy to be relieved of the burden of disposing those bicycles that were left unclaimed after having been stolen and retrieved.

After their first shipment to Tanzania in 2007, the cousins realised that relying on charitable funding would not create a viable business model. To provide an additional source of income, they opened a combined workshop-headquarters in the centre of Copenhagen, where they could repair second-hand bicycles and either sell them or hire them out to tourists.

The resulting revenue allowed Baisikeli to open a second workshop in Sierra Leone, where sales were boosted by a micro-loan scheme invented by a local bicycle mechanic. The scheme allows workers to buy the second-hand bicycles and pay for them over four to six months in instalments taken directly from their salary. As well as low-cost mobility, Baisikeli also provides an even more important long-term benefit: the transfer of knowledge and skills in fields such as bike mechanics, logistics and administration. This is a continuous process, as all Baisikeli's Danish employees spend some months every year working from Africa and exchange skills with their African colleagues. The goal is to develop a bicycle export industry in Africa.

To enable this, Baisikeli has started to produce custom-made bikes in Denmark, thereby developing the technical skills needed to start a bicycle industry from scratch - as it plans to do in Tanzania and Mozambique from 2011. The custom-made bicycles are then leased out to companies such as IKEA Denmark, and at the end of the lease (usually three years), the bicycles will be sent to Africa where local technicians will re-build them into three-wheeler hospital bikes.

IMPACT

By the end of 2010, more than 2,200 bikes had been shipped to Sierra Leone and Tanzania. The Masanga Hospital in Sierra Leone, which hosts one of Baisikeli's workshops, uses its bikes to support local micro-enterprise as well as to transport patients and medicine. Baisikeli also gained international recognition when it became the official bicycle provider to international conferences such as the Copenhagen Climate Conference (COP15) and Velo-City in 2010.

KEY LESSONS

GENERATING CHANGE THROUGH NETWORKS

Social innovation support

Baisikeli's founders had previous experience both as entrepreneurs and in development work, but they have also drawn on specialist social enterprise and innovation networks. One of the founders trained at Kaospilots, the Danish school of new business design and social innovation. Because his Baisikeli idea became an exam project at the school, they were able to get support from academic advisers and tap into wider knowledge networks. Additionally, the Danish Centre for the Social Economy, an independent support and advocacy organisation for the social enterprise sector, introduced them to helpful mentors. These support networks have been crucial in the development of the venture's concept.

THE EXPERIENCE OF PLACE

Creating broad appeal

Having a multi-use space (workshop/office/rental/retail) is not just economically effective but, more importantly, showcases the organisation's activities and ethic to the public. As well as generating income, the Copenhagen workshop communicates the entirety of Baisikeli's supply chain to tourists, residents, businesses and the national media. The workshop is thus integral to the business model – and, as a bonus, enriches the diversity of the city's retail environment.

RE-USING EXISTING ASSETS

A new purpose for waste

Giving new life to previously wasted resources – the old bikes that insurance companies normally have to pay to dispose of – is Baisikeli's core business proposition. The organisation has managed to join up this supply to a demand, closing the cycle of waste and providing training, jobs and low-cost mobility with a remarkably low environmental impact.

IN CONCLUSION

How do we discover new shared wealth in the very diverse types of waste we produce? Whilst the UK's improved recycling rates indicate how national and local policy makes a difference, the example of Baisikeli shows how entrepreneurial ventures can spot niches in waste flows and turn them into self-sustaining business models that create value across continents. Social venture intermediaries are a crucial enabler in unlocking such pathways.

OTHER EXAMPLES

Bike Works, Seattle, USA, 1996
...increases young people's mobility by teaching them repair skills and giving them a second-hand bicycle, which they pay back by doing community work; the city is aiming to triple bike usage between 2007 and 2017.

Union Cycle Works, London, UK, 2010
... is a not-for-profit co-operative cycling project housed in an old railway arch in Deptford, which trains homeless and unemployed people in repairing used bicycles, thereby increasing their mobility and employability.

First Step Trust: SMaRT, Salford, UK, 2005
...is a social enterprise garage service that repairs or dismantles and recycles abandoned cars, offering work placements and employment for young people and long-term unemployed adults.

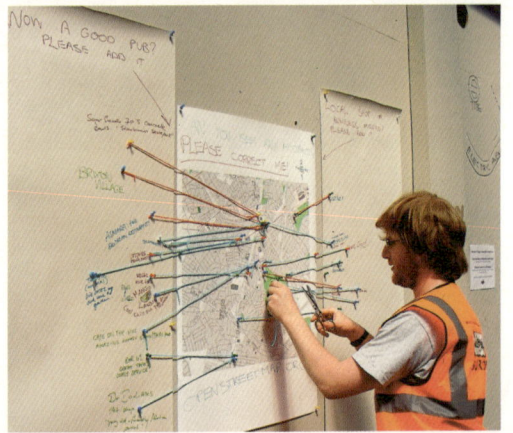

Bottom right: Mapping local ventures to help build Brixton Village. Other images: The result

03

BRIXTON VILLAGE

A SOCIABLE MARKET RE-START
LONDON, UNITED KINGDOM

'All along we've had this asset-based approach which said "this is not running on our talent and energy, this is running on the talent and energy of all the people who are coming in here." It's a DIY culture and we are there to act as a catalyst.'

Dougald Hine, Space Makers Agency

1 IN 5
BRIXTON
VILLAGE SHOPS
VACANT BEFORE
DECEMBER 2009

98 PROPOSALS
IN 1 WEEK

3 WEEKS TO
OPEN SHOPS

3 MONTHS RENT
FREE PERIOD

20
VACANT SHOPS
REVITALISED IN
DECEMBER 2009

CATALYSING A NEW APPROACH TO TOWN CENTRE ENTERPRISE

2008   **2009**   **2010**

HIGH VACANCY RATES & FAILED REDEVELOPMENT AMBITIONS

LANDOWNER REALISES THE VALUE OF SMALL-SCALE APPROACH

COUNCIL BROKERS CONTACT BETWEEN LAND-OWNER & SPACE MAKERS AGENCY (SMA)

PARTNERSHIP BETWEEN SMA & COUNCIL LEADS TO MUTUAL LEARNING

SPACE MAKERS AGENCY

LAND OWNERS SEED-FUND SMA

SMA SOCIAL MEDIA DRIVE TO GATHER IDEAS

LOCAL OUTREACH VIA PUB MEETINGS TO BUILD LOCAL TRUST

SWEAT EQUITY REFURBISHMENT OF SHOPS IN 3 WEEKS

SPACE EXPLORATION EVENT TO BUILD MOMENTUM

BRIXTON VILLAGE MARKET RE-OPENS WITH A RANGE OF NEW VENTURES

COMPETITION WITH 98 IDEAS SOURCED IN A SINGLE WEEK

BRIXTON VILLAGE HOLDS REGULAR EVENTS WITH CONTRIBUTIONS FROM TENANTS AND LOCALS

LOCAL ORGANISATION BRICK BOX TAKES OVER THE LEAD CATALYST ROLE

SMA STARTS NEW VENTURE IN WEST NORWOOD

A STALEMATE & LOCAL DISTRUST

BROKERING AN UNUSUAL PARTNERSHIP

CONFIGURING A SHARED PROCESS

AN OPEN PLATFORM FOR PARTICIPATION

EMBEDDING A NEW WAY OF DOING

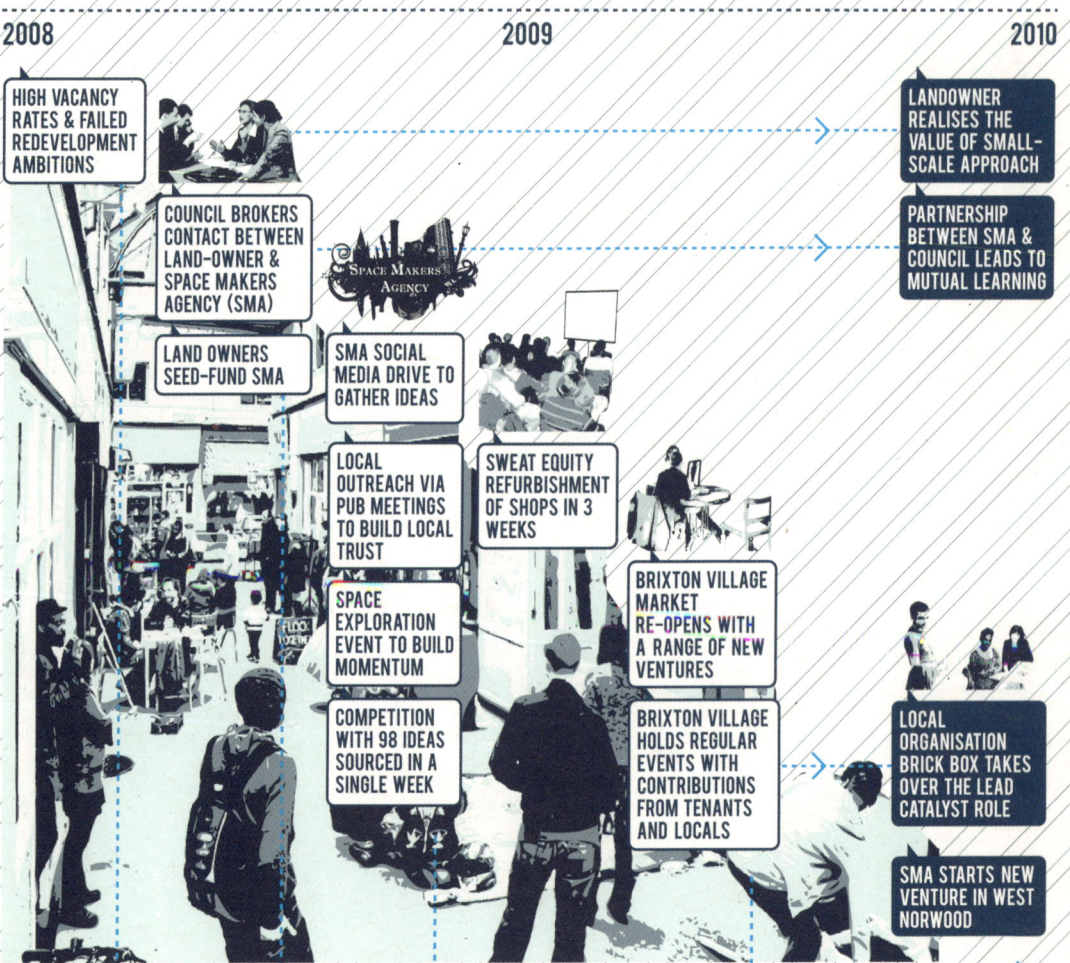

THE STORY

An alternative approach to retail revitalisation has succeeded where previous regeneration attempts by the council and landowners had failed. Space Makers Agency, a social enterprise, used an extensive personal network, a clear sense of direction and a savvy social media approach to create a buzz of activity and a pathway to a reborn, sociable market place.

In December 2008, with a fifth of the 100 units in Brixton Village standing vacant, the owners of this 1930s indoor market in South London proposed a major redevelopment of the site. This was resisted by local people who set up 'Friends of Brixton Market' to campaign for the conservation of the market. The owners withdrew their proposal in March 2009 and asked the local authority, Lambeth Council, for advice. Realising the need for an alternative to demolition, council regeneration officers suggested contacting Space Makers Agency, then recently founded.

A collective of highly motivated individuals with a track record as social entrepreneurs, Space Makers obtained a moderate sum of seed funding from the owners and invested a huge amount of personal time and energy into the project. With the explicit ambition of revitalising the market through small businesses and community initiative, the collective launched a social media drive to attract a wide range of people and ideas to what they termed 'the UK's biggest slack space project'.

Prompted by a blog, Twitter, Facebook and word of mouth, more than 350 people turned up to the initial 'Space Exploration' event in November 2009 to discuss new possibilities for the site. Space Makers gave interested people a week to come up with proposals for taking over a unit on an initial three-month rent-free lease. Within that week, Space Makers received 98 proposals, and selected 30, of which half were for short-term projects. After a month of minimal refurbishment work, the first of these units opened on 17 December 2009. The new ventures included vintage fashion boutiques, food stores, lantern-makers, furniture restorers, photographers, a children's magazine, a recycling workshop and a community shop run by groups such as Transition Town Brixton. In some cases up to three new businesses share as little as 10 sq m.

Space Makers facilitated weekly events to attract footfall and build a strong sense of direction, collective belonging and sociability. They also worked closely with community groups and with the established shopkeepers to increase local participation and feedback, and create a collaborative atmosphere. The gradual build-up of trust overcame some of the suspicion generated in the years before. This was crucial: Space Makers' intention was always to be a catalyst rather than a permanent manager of the market. After six months, shopkeepers and traders were encouraged to take over events and projects, and thus maintain the market as a sociable place in the town centre.

IMPACT

A year into the project, all 20 units are still occupied, seven of them by ventures originated in November 2009. Having shown the potential of a different approach to the landowners and the council, Space Makers have slowly withdrawn from the project and allowed it to become self-sustaining. A new local initiative, the Brick Box, has taken over one unit as an arts hub from where it continues the weekly events with the market traders. Over time Space Makers have built a genuine two-way learning relationship with Lambeth Council, already leading to a next project to revitalise vacant town centre spaces elsewhere.

KEY LESSONS

RECOGNISING THE PROTAGONISTS

Asset-holding civic entrepreneurs

Throughout the project Space Makers 'hosted' the revitalisation process. They were given significant freedom by both the landowners and Lambeth Council, whose previous proposals, based on demolition and redevelopment, had failed for lack of local support and trust. As networked and energetic outsiders with a clear sense of purpose, Space Makers took a hands-on role, formulating an alternative perspective for change that enabled them to create a coalition with local people and others with good ideas. Intensive outreach work, based on informal discussions online and regular open meetings in a nearby pub, was crucial to building trust and debating ideas widely. Tenants and other locals have been able to use these forums to suggest ideas for collaborative events, performances and stalls.

RE-USING EXISTING ASSETS

Recognising the potential

Space Makers' approach was based on recognising the potential of a space that was slated for redevelopment. Space Makers created a platform for activity and action to uncover what was possible and to get people working towards a shared purpose without a defined or designed state of 'completion'. Because of its tiny shop units and the fact that it was highly valued in the local community, the covered market could be brought to life through small enterprise and at relatively low cost, where a new development would have struggled to provide the small units that enable micro-businesses.

PARTICIPATION BEYOND CONSULTATION

An invitation to co-produce

Space Makers did not just offer an initial three-month rent-free lease to potential shopkeepers. More fundamentally they offered the possibility of being part of a movement to change the way the economy – and retail, in particular – works. Potential entrepreneurs were invited to be part of the project in a way that set it apart from the mainstream 'regeneration' discourse. This was attractive to Brixton's diverse communities, especially as a festival-like setting for creativity, food sharing and political debate complemented the shops. Continuous re-investment in this collective effort (through events, media articles, etc) was a core pillar under the project's success.

IN CONCLUSION

How do we open up fertile ground for small entrepreneurial ventures in our town centres? Where traditional regeneration approaches have often led to scaling and cloning, Brixton Village shows us an alternative: enabling diverse forms of entrepreneurship through activating social networks and a shared re-imagination of the possible. Crucially, a productive relation between private owners, the public sector and those offering this new perspective for change was at the heart of the venture.

OTHER EXAMPLES

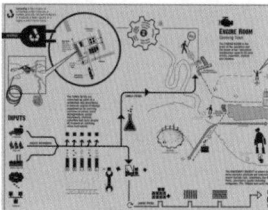

MeanWhile London: Opportunity Docks, London, UK, 2010
...was a competition to find 'meanwhile' uses for three sites in London's Royal Docks in the London Borough of Newham, next to a Olympic Games 2012 venue; image shows the Industri[us] project by a multidisciplinary team of Fluid and partners.

High Town Art For All, Luton, UK, 2010
...was an artists' collective that took over three vacant shops, facilitated by the Mean-while Project, to use as studios, workshops and spaces for exhibitions, poetry evenings, and training sessions for local businesses.

Landshare, UK, 2009
...is a web-based platform connecting more than 57,000 people who have vacant land to share with people who want land for cultivating food.

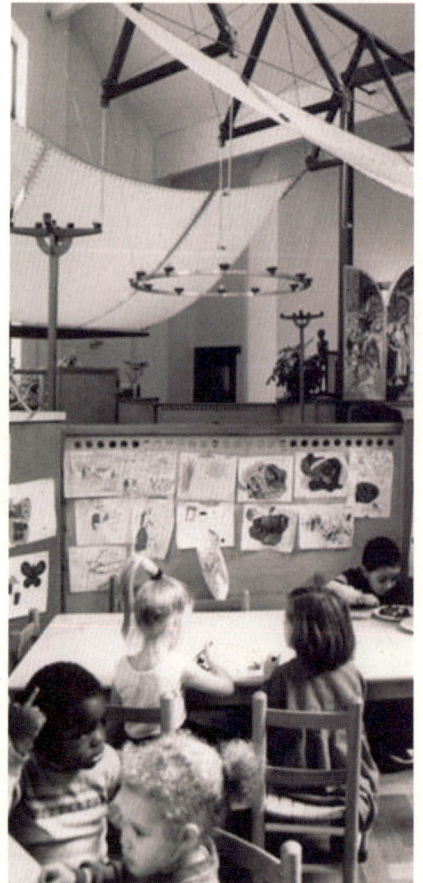

Top: Entrance to the Health Centre. Bottom left: Summer fayre in the public gardens created on a wasteland. Bottom right: Crèche day in the Church Hall, 1980s

04

BROMLEY BY BOW CENTRE

A PLATFORM FOR NEIGHBOURHOOD WELL-BEING
LONDON, UNITED KINGDOM

'Our business model is perhaps a bit unusual. Most business consultants would advise you to pick one or two things and specialise in them. But in an area like this, people's needs aren't particularly specialised, so that doesn't work for us. So instead we offer a holistic range of services for the people in Bromley by Bow.'

Susie Dye, Programmes Development Officer, Bromley by Bow Centre

12
PEOPLE IN CHURCH CONGREGATION IN 1984

2,000
WEEKLY USERS OF CENTRE IN 2010

28
SUCCESSFUL SOCIAL ENTERPRISES CATALYSED SINCE 2005 GENERATING OVER **200** NEW JOBS

BUILDING A HOLISTIC PLACE FOR HEALTH, SKILLS, JOBS AND NEW INITIATIVES

1950 — 1980 — 1985 — 1990 — 1995 — 2000 — 2005 — 2010

01 HALL BUILT IN 1800S

02 CHURCH BUILT IN 1957

NEW MINISTER ARRIVES

CHURCH & HALL OPEN FOR USE BY LOCAL PEOPLE

03 HEALTH CENTRE OPENS

04 CAFE AND EXTENSION OPENS

05 ENTERPRISE BARN OPENS

* EXTENSION: CAFE, COMMUNITY SPACE, POTTERY & STONE CARVING WORKSHOPS AND OFFICE SPACE

* ENTERPRISE BARN: AFFORDABLE SPACE FOR SOCIAL ENTERPRISE START-UPS

* HALL: USED FOR SOCIAL ACTIVITES AND WORKSHOPS

* PUBLIC GARDENS: CREATED AND MAINTAINED BY LOCAL VOLUNTEERS

* SURGERY: RECEPTION SPACE USED AS INFORMAL COMMUNITY SPACE AND GALLERY

* RECEPTION: HEALTH, HOUSING, EDUCATION & SOCIAL SERVICES SHARE SPACE

* CHURCH SPACE: RELIGIOUS WORSHIP, CRECHE & THEATRE / PERFORMING ARTS

THE STORY

Creating a culture that encourages people to come forward with ideas has helped turn an underused church and its ancillary premises into a hugely popular local asset. A new minister decided to open the hall up for community use, and created a base for a wide range of initiatives. Incrementally, this has grown into a revolutionary organisation.

The Bromley by Bow United Reform Church in East London had a congregation of just 12 people and almost no funds when the Rev Andrew Mawson arrived in 1984. Faced with a near empty church in a low-income neighbourhood, the minister and his congregation decided to open up the church hall to the community, primarily in response to informal conversations with local residents who needed space for a range of purposes.

Amongst the first users were a carpentry workshop, a woman who needed somewhere to build a boat and a dance teacher. The range of activities soon expanded to include various community services and small enterprises. The hall was offered free of charge to projects that helped address local needs; artists who wanted studio space could pay in kind by offering workshops to local people.

In this beginning phase, what was crucial was not raising money but rather building purpose together with a wider group of users and re-embedding the asset in the community as a trusted and useful resource.

Plans to start a nursery led to a total refurbishment of the 200-seat church. The new space comprised a 40-seat sanctuary, the nursery, a gallery, a theatre space and a flexible community room. While regular worship continued, an increasing variety of secular projects in and outside the church premises drew in a considerable group of volunteers, and Mawson was able to gather a team around him who helped to drive further growth. The Bromley by Bow Centre was established as an independent registered charity in 1994.

The tragic death of a local resident who slipped through the gaps in local health and social services provision prompted the team to consider the role that a genuinely community-embedded organisation could play in improving people's lives. In 1997, they set up an integrated health centre on the derelict land surrounding the church. This covered multiple aspects of health and well-being by combining a public park with a GP practice that is deeply integrated into the social enterprise, a families project, a social landlords' office and other local services.

Mawson has since moved on, co-founding the Community Action Network to promote the role of entrepreneurship in building communities, and creating the Water City Festival as part of a wider vision to reconnect East London neighbourhoods to the waterways in the area. Meanwhile, the centre has continued to evolve and flourish. As the scale of community activities has grown, in-house social enterprises have been set up to help fund them.

IMPACT

The Bromley by Bow Centre is widely recognised as an exemplar of how community centres can transform separate services into a cherished place in the neighbourhood. Many initial projects have developed into independent (social) enterprises, including a nursery and artists' studios. The centre has also brought in grant funding from the private and public sectors and from the National Lottery, for enterprising projects with a focus on supporting and investing in excluded people. For example, mental health service users help to maintain the green spaces. Annual turnover now exceeds £4 million, and there are more than 100 staff members, the majority of whom are local. The centre hosts more than 2,000 people every week and has become the third largest provider of adult education and training in the borough of Tower Hamlets.

KEY LESSONS

RECOGNISING THE PROTAGONISTS

Asset-holding civic entrepreneurs

In the initial phase, the minister's attitude was crucial: he was prepared to offer the asset he controlled for anything that seemed a valuable idea. Free from the obligation to maximise revenue, instead of asking for rent, he asked people to work together and co-produce their concepts for local benefit. This built the most important currency needed: trust. Mawson could do this because he had the local support and organisational authority to assess the risks and opportunities, and give permission locally, instead of at an abstract bureaucratic level. This created fertile ground for a host of initiatives and gradually attracted a team of people who grew the centre's activities.

RE-USING EXISTING ASSETS

People make a place

The centre built on existing assets: an underused building was brought to life by local people's ideas and skills. With the blessing of the congregation, the church premises were re-imagined as a multi-use space with both secular and multi-faith events. This became an on-going invitation for people to use it for their ideas, maximising the use value of the building. A broader agenda for change thus emerged organically from the initial engagements with local people. Development decisions were made as opportunities emerged, instead of through a plan-led approach. The centre is now led by a professional team but still maintains its strong local roots, close relationships and ever-evolving approach.

THE EXPERIENCE OF PLACE

Inclusion and well-being

As the centre expanded, a space was created that communicates to users that they are highly valued. A single architect worked with the centre to ensure that each phase integrated with the whole. The design focuses on inviting people in, and on multi-functionality. A space for worship has been maintained as a smaller but integral element of the site; the garden and café are open to all, and health and housing services share the same reception space – which is no institutional waiting room but a place where locals can meet informally. Together with a gallery and events space, and a self-maintained green space with allotments, this has helped the centre emanate a holistic sense of well-being.

IN CONCLUSION

How do we move from a public service model that focuses on providing for peoples' needs to one that embraces their strengths and liberates their skills, ideas, energy and drive? A key step is to move from single-function public services to places for integrated neighbourhood delivery. The Bromley by Bow Centre also shows that this is how we should view physical assets, recognising that their use value depends on the frontline staff breathing life into them.

OTHER EXAMPLES

The Park Local Opportunity Centre, Bristol, UK, 2000
...is a community hub that grew out of a former secondary school and now offers a variety of services, activities and business opportunities to the local community.

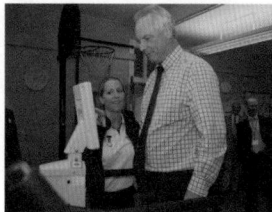

Central Surrey Health, Epsom, UK, 2006
...is one of the first employee co-owned social enterprises within the NHS, spun out of the local Primary Care Trust. It is a not-for-profit organisation that provides community nursing and therapy services to the people of central Surrey.

The Hill, Abergavenny, UK, 2009
...is a coalition of third and public sector organisations that responded to the closure of a local tertiary college. After extensive community activism, they managed to retain the site for community use, providing innovative educational services for young and old.

Shop front of the Brooklyn Superhero Supply Co. featuring a choice of capes and magic potions

BROOKLYN SUPERHERO SUPPLY CO.

A TUTORING CENTRE ON THE HIGH STREET
NEW YORK, UNITED STATES

'We may operate behind a store that sells gravity by the pound, superhero capes or pirate peg legs, but we're serious about student writing.'

826 National

2,077
STUDENTS SERVED
IN 2009 / 2010

800
VOLUNTEERS

90
BOOKS
PUBLISHED
IN 2009/2010

LOWERING THE THRESHOLDS TO LEARNING AND VOLUNTEERING

05 COMMUNITY OF LOCAL WRITERS WORKING IN PUBLISHING

IN-HOUSE PUBLISHING OF CHILDREN'S CREATIVE WORK

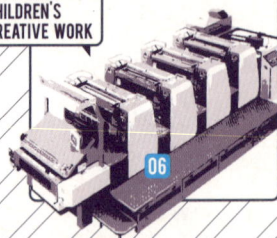

06

03 SECRET DOORWAY BEHIND BOOKCASE LEADS TO READING & TUTORING SPACE

OFFICE & PRESS

05

WRITER

CHILDREN'S BOOKS AND MAGAZINES ARE PRINTED

06

TUTORING SPACE

04

LOCAL WRITERS AS MENTORS TO LOCAL CHILDREN

03

SHOP

02

STUDENT

STORIES ARE SOLD IN SHOP **07**

01

WRITER

STUDENT

04

TUTORING SPACE PROVIDES LEARNING ENVIRONMENT FOR LOCAL CHILDREN

THE SHOP IS A 'FRONT' FOR THE ORGANISATION AND ALSO CONTRIBUTES FINANCIAL SUPPORT

02

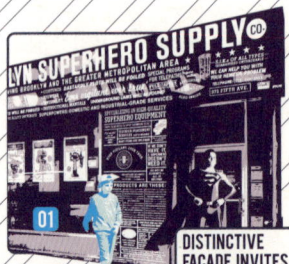

01 DISTINCTIVE FACADE INVITES CURIOSITY

STORIES WRITTEN BY CHILDREN ARE PRINTED & SOLD IN THE SHOP

07

THE STORY

The Brooklyn Superhero Supply Co. in New York City is a small shop selling all types of superhero gear from photon shooters to invisibility potions. However, hidden behind a trick bookshelf is 826NYC, part of a network of non-profit organisations supporting young people with their writing skills. The place creates a magic experience integrated in the everyday of a shopping street in Brooklyn, and extends a highly original invitation to participate – both to potential volunteers and to youngsters.

The Brooklyn Superhero Supply Co. is modelled on the Pirate Supply Store in San Francisco, which was established in 2002. The concept was the outcome of pure serendipity. Dave Eggers was looking for a venue to house the fledgling tutoring centre that he wanted to create. He saw this as a place where the many local writers he knew – most of whom worked flexible hours – could spend some of their spare time to fulfil a need of which he had become increasingly aware: for one-on-one tutoring for children who struggle in school. They found an attractive space on 826 Valencia Street that his small publishing company and the tutoring centre could share, but were told the address was exclusively zoned for retail. Instead of looking for a new site, they decided to make the front of the building into a pirate's shop that would appeal to their target audience of 6-to-18-year-olds.

Initially, this highly unusual proposition had to overcome some understandable suspicion from parents, teachers and children. When a friend of Eggers, the educator Nínive Calegari, got involved she managed to connect the writers' community to that of teachers and parents. Soon, it showed that the magic and whimsy worked to connect the tutoring centre with the community: its culture of creativity and adventure helped to attract curious locals as potential volunteers, and children for whom this place was clearly different than school or other places associated with 'being helped'.

The pirate store front also proved to be a success as it added a vital stream of revenue to the non-profit organisation. When 826NYC was opened in 2004 as the second '826' venture, it was purposely built with the Brooklyn Superhero Supply Co. as a front. Other 826 chapters have since opened in six other US cities, each with a unique store front (examples include the Greater Boston Bigfoot Research Institute, Los Angeles' Echo Park Time Travel Mart, the Greenwood Space Travel Supply Company in Seattle, and the Liberty Street Robot Supply and Repair in Ann Arbor). All of the chapters are located in communities with socially and economically diverse populations; their locations include high streets, shopping malls and residential areas. As the concept spread, the umbrella organisation 826 National was established in order to support chapters and facilitate knowledge exchange between them.

826NYC relies on more than 800 volunteers to provide a wide variety of free programmes and services, including after-school drop-in tutoring and fieldtrips that end with students taking away their own published book. Many of the volunteers have professional writing experience; others are simply fascinated by the store, and offer their time role-playing as superhero assistants in the shop. 826NYC's work also extends into local schools, where support is offered to teachers in the form of in-class tutoring assistance and help with special projects.

IMPACT

There are currently eight 826 chapters in cities across the USA. Together they provide almost 24,000 students a year with tutoring, thanks to more than 5,000 volunteers. More than 850 publishing projects are produced annually with contributions from students between the eight chapters. Several US educator groups are currently hoping to become part of the 826 network, and there have been inquiries from groups in Canada and Mexico. Across the Atlantic, several tutoring centres in the UK and Ireland have been inspired by the work of 826 National.

KEY LESSONS

THE EXPERIENCE OF PLACE

An atmosphere of magic potential

The store fronts of 826 chapters are a central aspect of their success: they establish an ambient culture of non-institutional fun and creative achievement. Students' writings figure among the products on sale in the shops, which provide the organisation with welcome revenue, though their real advantage is in creating a very original interface with the public. They reduce barriers to participation by removing the stigma often associated with tutoring spaces and have become a kind of community venture where people can 'wander in' and join in the magic. This supports the volunteer recruitment process, and produces an environment that engenders creativity and high quality engagement.

GENERATING CHANGE THROUGH NETWORKS

Collective capacity to grow

Local educators and community workers are the ones who initiate the setting-up of 826 chapters. Responding to different conditions, chapters have opened in various neighbourhood settings. Often, they are based on existing tutoring organisations looking for new directions, which means that they can connect to local expertise while also drawing upon the knowledge, experience and fundraising capacities of 826 National. The umbrella organisation helps with strategic concept development, creates collective fundraising capacity and encourages exchange between the chapters.

PARTICIPATION BEYOND CONSULTATION

Co-producing tangible products

826 does not just ask the children and young people what they would like to do but offers them a wide range of opportunities and guidance, as writers and publishers sit shoulder-to-shoulder with the young people. Moreover, it focuses on making outcomes tangible: students' work is published in newspapers, magazines, and books, some of them sponsored by well-known authors. 826NYC's outreach programmes have also been a substantial success. Beyond allowing the organisation to reach a high number of children, they also help to forge alliances with teachers, thereby establishing a platform for collaboration between the tutoring centre and its community.

IN CONCLUSION

The Brooklyn Superhero Supply Co. shows how a magic intervention can cut right across formal land-use restrictions and, through surprise and delight, can achieve unique outcomes. It reveals that if we embed mutual teaching and learning at the heart of our places, the town, village or urban neighbourhood can become the school rather than be separated from it.

OTHER EXAMPLES

Hoxton Street Monster Supplies, London, UK, 2010
...is the eerie store front for the Ministry of Stories, a teaching centre co-founded by author Nick Hornby, inspired by 826 Valencia.

Hackney Pirates, London, UK, 2010
...is an out-of-school educational hub that started by offering week-long creative workshops during the summer vacation.

Fighting Words, Dublin, Ireland, 2008
...is a creative writing centre set up by novelist Roddy Doyle, inspired by 826 Valencia but without a shop. The centre contains one big, playful open-plan space with revolving bookshelves inviting in students of all ages for free tutoring.

Eddie Kirkby from Fab Lab and Australian rugby player Matt King examine the prototype for a light-weight beach cricket bat

FAB LAB MANCHESTER

A 21ST CENTURY MANUFACTURING WORKSHOP
MANCHESTER, UNITED KINGDOM

'The main aim is for people to have the power to solve their own problems, rather than have to go to a shop and get something that is only 50% suitable for their need.'

Eddie Kirkby, Operations Support Manager, The Manufacturing Institute

£35,000
SET-UP COST OF EQUIPMENT

1,800
VISITORS IN FIRST
9 MONTHS

5 PATENTS

15 NEW PRODUCTS DEVELOPED

GROWING A GLOBAL NETWORK OF LOCAL INNOVATION AND PRODUCTION SPACES

2002 · **2005** · **2011**

MIT LAUNCHES FIRST LAB IN BOSTON

OUTREACH IN LOCAL AREA

MIT AND PARTNERS INTEGRATED INTO FAB LAB NETWORK

LOOSE PROTOCOL / OPEN BRAND OF FAB LAB FRANCHISE

VIRAL GROWTH IN POPULARITY FUELS GROWTH IN NETWORK

NETWORK CONTINUES TO GROW GLOBALLY

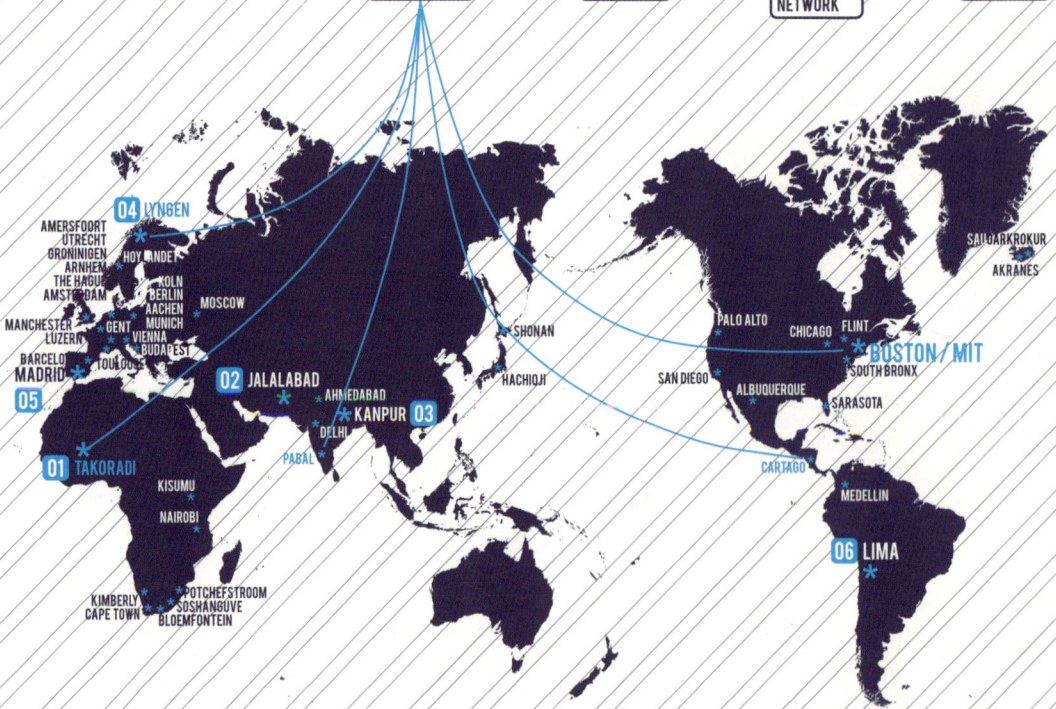

Map labels:

04 LYNGEN
AMERSFOORT
UTRECHT
GRONINIGEN
ARNHEM
THE HAGUE
AMSTERDAM
HOY ANDET
KOLN
BERLIN
AACHEN
MUNICH
MOSCOW
MANCHESTER
LUZERN
GENT
VIENNA
BUDAPEST
BARCELONA
MADRID
TOULOUSE
05
01 TAKORADI
02 JALALABAD
AHMEDABAD
KANPUR 03
DELHI
PABAL
KISUMU
NAIROBI
SHONAN
HACHIOJI
PALO ALTO
CHICAGO
FLINT
BOSTON / MIT
SOUTH BRONX
SAN DIEGO
ALBUQUERQUE
SARASOTA
CARTAGO
MEDELLIN
06 LIMA
SAUDARKROKUR
AKRANES
KIMBERLY
CAPE TOWN
POTCHEFSTROOM
SOSHANGUVE
BLOEMFONTEIN

01 'FU-FU' POUNDER THAT HARNESSES SOLAR POWER TO MAKE ELECTRICITY TO COOK FOOD

02 FAB-FI; A WI-FI NETWORK MADE FROM RECYCLED AID EQUIPMENT

03 MILK QUALITY TESTING DEVICE

04 ELECTRONIC SHEEP-TRACKING DEVICE

05 FAB LAB HOUSE THAT PRODUCES MORE ENERGY THAN IT CONSUMES

06 CARDBOARD SHREDDER AND MILK CARTON RECYCLER

THE STORY

Fab Lab Manchester is a place where everyone can get engaged in product design and development. A modern-day manufacturing workshop with equipment that ranges from a 3D printer to a computerised embroidery machine, it reverses the traditional approach to producing consumer goods by empowering communities, students, individuals and SMEs to do it themselves.

The first Fab Lab (short for fabrication laboratory) was established as a community outreach programme by Neil Gerschenfeld at the Massachusetts Institute for Technology (MIT) in 2002. The simplicity of the idea – though enabled by sophisticated technology – tapped into an emerging cultural trend of self-production; it had instant appeal. Initially, a group of universities that worked together with MIT showed interest in adopting the idea; soon, a wide range of non-academic organisations also saw its potential. There are now close to 50 Fab Labs across the world.

Manchester was the first UK city to host a Fab Lab. It was set up by the Manufacturing Institute, a charity that works to advance manufacturing in the North-West of England. Its trustees saw the Fab Lab as a way of sparking renewed interest in manufacturing as a viable and attractive activity, and to promote Manchester as an innovative city. Manchester City Council also saw the potential of the proposition, as did Manchester Knowledge Capital, a university-backed innovation network, and the Manchester Innovation Investment Fund. The latter agreed to provide 15 months of start-up funding. Fab Lab Manchester opened in March 2010, on the ground floor of the 'Chips Building', in a high-profile regeneration area. The space was zoned for commercial activities; agreeing a flexible (two-year) lease and getting the space ready for occupation took less than two months.

The Fab Lab encourages the creation of everyday objects as well as the development of new ideas. It offers equipment for anything from wood-cutting to the production of circuit-boards and 3D models. It is open to businesses as well as members of the public, thereby creating space for both professionals and for an amateur economy. Fridays and Saturdays are 'Open Lab' days, when non-commercial users – families, individuals, students and schools – can use the facilities free of charge. Users who might not have showed up independently are encouraged to do so through community outreach programmes set up in collaboration with educational institutions and other social entrepreneurs (such as the nearby MadLab). The rest of the week, the laboratory is reserved for commercial users who can rent out the entire Lab, thereby ensuring confidentiality for product development whilst cross-subsidising the Open Labs.

The Fab Lab actively advocates collaborative learning. Online platforms facilitate the exchange of knowledge and experience between Fab Lab users across the world, while within each Lab people are encouraged to document their work for future reference and to teach others how to handle equipment. Individuals are provided with advice on patenting their inventions; and they can also book the Lab for further product development.

IMPACT

In its first nine months Fab Lab Manchester received more than 1,800 visits and spawned a wealth of inventions including an MP3-toothbrush, a beach cricket bat and a baby's bottle that changes colour when the milk reaches the right temperature. But all types of production are welcome, and many users make and take home everyday objects such as furniture, ornaments or board games. Much more than a pure R&D and fabrication workshop, the Fab Lab has also started to function as a leisure destination. Older people who bring their grandchildren to the Lab for recreation can stay there to work or read the paper; students hang out with their peers – and there have even been cases where young couples have met for a date at the Fab Lab.

KEY LESSONS

PARTICIPATION BEYOND CONSULTATION

THE EXPERIENCE OF PLACE

GENERATING CHANGE THROUGH NETWORKS

An invitation to DIY

The Fab Lab taps into the same culture that created MySpace and YouTube: people with the desire to develop and create their own ideas and products, and share them with others. By offering a physical platform to enable this, Fab Lab challenges negative perceptions of manufacturing as 'outmoded' or of product development as a highly technical process, inaccessible to the general public.

A 'play' aesthetic

Thanks to powerful backers and landowners willing to experiment, Fab Lab Manchester could push the boundaries of what is commonly understood as mixed use, offering a new type of activity to a regenerated community by occupying regular retail premises. The physical space communicates this purpose through an inviting aesthetic that combines a 'play ethic' with high-tech opportunities. Combining the work/research area with a social and informal meeting space helps to break down barriers to participation while also encouraging an informal exchange of ideas and know-how.

Global and local links

The Fab Lab is a strong brand but one that can easily be appropriated and adapted across the world. Although all Fab Labs have to sign up to a 'Fab Charter', there are no formal requirements to joining the network. The original MIT Fab Lab supports aspiring initiatives by recommending equipment and connecting them to existing Labs to facilitate shared learning. Locally, a crucial enabling factor for the Fab Lab Manchester was the brokering role of the Manufacturing Institute and the City Council, which both saw an opportunity to add to their ambitions for the manufacturing sector and the city.

IN CONCLUSION

If so many agree that our society needs to make things again, how do we embed this in the everyday life of our places? By developing the new living libraries that offer access to know-how, inspiration and the tools for physical as well as digital creation. What Fab Lab suggests is that these new learning and doing institutions form a new class of essential neighbourhood social infrastructure, plugged into global networks but adopted and adapted through local collaboration.

OTHER EXAMPLES

London Hackspace, London, UK, 2010
...is a community-run 'hackerspace' where people can come to share tools and knowledge. It is open to members 24 hours a day, has a swap shop for unwanted electronic equipment and holds regular free open evenings and workshops.

TechShop, San Francisco, USA, 2006
...is a workspace where, for a monthly fee, individuals and SMEs alike can use an array of advanced equipment to produce anything from robots to cooling-systems.

MadLab, Manchester, UK, 2009
...is a workspace where creative people can get together to collaborate on projects as well as present and discuss their ideas; it collaborates on events with Fab Lab.

A local orchestra plays at the inauguration of the Earlsburn wind farm, before local residents put their signatures on their wind turbine

07

FINTRY DEVELOPMENT TRUST

A COMMUNITY-PRIVATE ENERGY PARTNERSHIP
FINTRY, UNITED KINGDOM

'If, a number of years down the line, we have solved all the energy issues of the village, then who knows what could happen?'

Gordon Cowtan, co-founder, Fintry Development Trust

£140,000
FUNDS DISTRIBUTED IN THE FIRST YEAR AFTER WIND TURBINE COMPLETION

21
MICRO RENEWABLES PROJECTS ENABLED

£600
SAVINGS PER HOUSEHOLD PARTICIPATING IN FREE INSULATION SCHEME

REALISING THE BENEFITS OF A PARTNERSHIP APPROACH

ENERGY & HEATING UPGRADE FOR LOCAL SPORTS CLUB AND COMMUNITY HALL

FREE ENERGY SURVEY AND HOME INSULATION FOR OVER HALF OF LOCAL HOMES

FREE HOUSEHOLD MICRO-RENEWABLES ADVICE

CAR-SHARING CLUB WITH VOUCHER SYSTEM

CREATION OF COMMUNITY ORCHARD AND ALLOTMENTS

HOSTING OF REGIONAL RENEWABLE ENERGY FAIR

WELCOME!

ASPIRATION: ACQUISITION OF LOCAL PUB & OTHER COMMUNITY ASSETS

THE FINTRY DEVELOPMENT TRUST MODEL

OTHER COMMUNITY BENEFIT MODELS THROUGHOUT THE UK AND WHAT THEY HAVE ACHIEVED

CEFN CROES WIND FARM COMMUNITY TRUST
NEW PLAYGROUND, COMMUNITY TRANSPORT, LOCAL HERITAGE & WOODLAND RESTORATION, SCHOOL EQUIPMENT

VECTIS WIND FARM LOCAL ENERGY ORGANISATION
GREEN ENERGY RATE, REBATE FOR LOCAL RESIDENTS

ENERGY4ALL
SHARE OFFERS FOR CO-OP WITH MINORITY STAKE IN WIND FARM, FULLY CO-OPERATIVELY OWNED WIND FARMS

one share

BURTON WOLD COMMUNITY FUND
INTEREST-FREE LOANS FOR ENERGY SAVINGS PROJECTS, LIBRARY BOOK PURCHASES, ENERGY SAVINGS, INFORMATION POINT

STRATHDEARN COMMUNITY BENEFIT FUND & CHARITABLE TRUST
FURTHER EDUCATION AND TRAINING, GRANTS TO YOUNG PEOPLE, EVENTS FOR SENIOR CITIZENS, NEW SPORTS FACILITIES

THE STORY

In 2008, the village of Fintry, in Stirlingshire, saw the first fruits of an unusual wind energy partnership. Rather than taking a not-in-my-back-yard view of the proposed Earlsburn wind farm development in the Fintry Hills, the village had asked the developer to build one more turbine and allow the community to buy it over time, financed by the sales of the energy it produced. A wide range of local projects has already been financed through this locally generated income. As such, Fintry is part of a growing group of partnerships between companies and communities showing how cross-sector collaboration can work in practice.

Though less than 15 miles north of Glasgow, Fintry is not on the main gas network, instead relying on expensive oil, electricity and solid fuels for heating and cooking. This led to very high bills and exposure to price volatility, causing fuel poverty and uncertainty – and leading some of the local residents to search for alternatives. When the developer Falck Renewables lodged its proposal for the nearby 14 turbine wind farm with the community council, they immediately spotted an opportunity for a joint venture.

Falck had already deployed community share offer deals elsewhere in Britain through the co-operative energy company Energy4All. Fintry, however, was proposing something more unusual and, in the residents' eyes, more democratic: a community asset, managed by a local trust, which could generate benefits for the entire village,

not just for those who could afford to buy shares. After protracted negotiations, Falck agreed, allowing the Fintry Development Trust to buy the 15th turbine over a 15-year period. The electricity the turbine provides is sold to the National Grid and any profits left once the mortgage and maintenance payments have been made, go to the village. As a result, the communally run sports club and more than half of Fintry's homes have benefited from a free survey and insulation project paid from profits made so far and run by the Energy Agency, a regional not-for-profit organisation. This has had palpable effects on the household budgets of those taking part, saving them on average £600 per year.

Also, while most of the villagers had not been very involved in the early negotiations with Falck – they were generally happy to let the initiators and community council take the lead – they have since taken to the idea of energy saving, which has led to further financial benefits. The trust now supports an adviser on domestic-level heat and energy generation, leading to 21 micro-energy schemes so far.

The trust has also started a car club as an experiment, giving all residents tradable vouchers to encourage ride-sharing. Furthermore, it is looking into creating a community allotment and orchard, and branching into other ventures that could create economic or social returns. In 2009, Fintry held its first renewable energy fair, inviting people and organisations from across Scotland to join the discussion and exchange experiences and know-how.

IMPACT

Within a year, the wind energy partnership generated a £140,000 return for the village, and once the mortgage on the turbine is paid off, annual profits are estimated to rise to £400,000-£500,000 for the rest of its 25-year lifespan. The insulation project alone has saved the 800-strong community at least £90,000 a year, as well as reducing CO_2 emissions by 464 tons a year. Through the fair and informal contacts, the village now also advises other communities on similar projects, and the success of this and other ventures has led the on-shore wind energy industry to create a community benefit protocol to encourage such collaborative practice.

KEY LESSONS

RECOGNISING THE PROTAGONISTS

A community-private partnership

The crucial elements of this partnership were a group of proactive villagers – a mix of long-term residents and newcomers – and the developers. Initially it was the community council, despite having few formal powers and only a small budget, that formed the platform that could connect the two parties. Realising it needed local support for the proposal, Falck Renewables responded to the community's requests, which had been clearly articulated before the planning stage. Support from the community council and the local MSP was also instrumental in this process. Beyond this, the role of the public sector has been limited. Nimbyism has been minimal – helped by the fact that the wind farm is four miles away but also by proactive communication and leadership on the issue.

PARTICIPATION BEYOND CONSULTATION

Co-producing local benefits

It is becoming increasingly clear that wind farms may not be acceptable to localities unless proceeds and benefits are also shared locally – but how this happens is shaped by local negotiations as well as the role of national organisations such as Energy4All. A wide range of benefit models now exists across the UK, from co-operative-owned wind farms to schemes that encourage households to take an equity stake in projects in return for yearly returns, and trusts that distribute funds to local projects and groups. In the case of Fintry, the early experiences with the Development Trust have also given the community confidence and capacity to apply for grant funding to complement locally generated income for some of their activities, based on a shared direction of travel defined by the wind farm project.

RECOGNISING WHERE VALUE LIES

Regulatory hurdles to self-provision

Whilst the village clearly benefits from reduced energy use and shared income, it has not yet achieved its ambition to become self-reliant through a local energy services company. It had hoped that, through bulk-buying energy and reselling it locally, it could finance a collective micro-generation infrastructure but complying with existing regulations would have made such a local utilities venture too expensive. Instead, the trust employed a dedicated energy adviser who has enabled more than 20 domestic-scale projects in the village, ranging from heat pumps to biomass heating systems.

IN CONCLUSION

How can private development proposals benefit local people in a way that genuinely builds community prosperity over the long term? The assertive approach of Fintry's residents created a mutually beneficial outcome; it shows how community-private partnerships can create shared assets for common use, increasing the community's financial literacy as well as strengthening its economic and environmental resilience.

OTHER EXAMPLES

Baywind Energy Co-operative, Cumbria, UK, 1996
...is an industrial and provident society that has funded the building of six wind turbines by selling shares to local people, who have to date enjoyed a 7% annual return on their investment.

Ballen / Brundby Straw-fired District Heating, Samsø, Denmark, 2004
...is the only 100% consumer-owned heating plant on the island which over 7 years has succeeded in relying solely on renewable energy sources.

Ecotricity, Stroud, UK, 2005
...is a green energy company that invests a large part of its earnings in building new wind turbines across the UK; in seven years, it has put nearly £50 million into wind energy and other renewables.

The sign above the entrance to what is now much more than a local pub

08

THE GEORGE AND DRAGON

A COMMUNITY-OWNED PUB / SHOP / LIBRARY
HUDSWELL, UNITED KINGDOM

'When we decided to take over the George and Dragon, it wasn't just a question of getting our pub back and maintaining the status quo. It was about new and bigger aspirations for the village as a whole, about better shared facilities, and a wish to create a space where people can carry out new projects and activities.'

Martin Booth, co-founder, Hudswell Co-operative

82
OF THE VILLAGE'S
200 RESIDENTS
AS INVESTORS

30
YEARS SINCE THE
VILLAGE LAST HAD
A GROCERY SHOP

3x3
SIZE OF THE
LITTLE SHOP IN
METRES

CO-INVESTING IN THE HEART OF THE VILLAGE

AUGUST 2008

THE GEORGE & DRAGON OFFICIALLY CLOSES

JULY 2009

VILLAGE HALL MEETING IS HELD ABOUT THE FUTURE OF THE PUB

OCTOBER 2009

THE LOCAL OFFER TO TAKE OVER THE PUB IS ACCEPTED

FEBRUARY 2010

HUDSWELL CO-OP GETS THE KEYS TO THE PUB

JUNE 2010

THE GEORGE & DRAGON OFFICIALLY RE-OPENS AFTER REFURBISHMENT

DECEMBER 2010

THE LITTLE SHOP OPENS

FIRST FLOOR SPACE PLANNED FOR B&B

THE GEORGE & DRAGON PUB

SMALL VILLAGE LIBRARY

THE LITTLE SHOP

VILLAGERS GROW VEGETABLES ON ADJACENT ALLOTMENTS

VILLAGE EVENTS INCLUDING BBQ & FOLK DANCING ON THE PUB PATIO

KIDS SCARECROW COMPETITION IN THE PUB GARDENS

TOURISTS USING THE FREE WI-FI TO FIND THEIR WAY

WEEKLY BOOK CLUB IN DINING ROOM & LIBRARY

NEW HIKING TRAIL BUILT BY LOCAL VOLUNTEERS

GROCERY & PACKAGE DROP-OFF POINT STAFFED BY VOLUNTEERS

THE STORY

When the recession forced the George and Dragon public house in Hudswell to close down in 2008, the North Yorkshire village lost not only its only pub but the very heart of its social life. However, through forming a co-operative to take over the old pub, residents created a vibrant community hub – with allotments, a library and the village's first grocery in more than 30 years.

In early 2009, after the George and Dragon pub had lain empty for six months, there seemed to be little interest from potential buyers. Inspired by a seminar on community shares, local resident Martin Booth called together a group of villagers to discuss the potential for taking over the pub themselves. In July, a town meeting in the village hall attracted 45 residents, who showed strong enthusiasm and support for the project.

The Hudswell Community Pub co-operative was set up and made a formal offer to buy the George and Dragon at the advertised price of £209,950. However, it took time – and pressure from the local media, spurred on by the villagers – to persuade the owner, who was from outside the region, to accept this offer.

Over the following six months, the co-op set out to raise the £220,000 needed to buy the pub. To keep it a community affair, the co-op rules stipulate that at least 40% of investors have to reside in the parish. However, the villagers also knew they were unlikely to raise enough capital within the parish alone, and therefore leveraged local media, the internet and word of mouth to create awareness of their project. By February 2010, the co-op had 169 members, of whom 79 were locals; other members were mostly friends and relatives of local residents but also regular visitors or sympathisers from throughout the region. But the investment prospectus also showed this was not to be seen as charitable giving: members are estimated to make an annual return of between 3.5% and 5% on their investment. In total, it raised almost a quarter of a million pounds through investments and grants, and built a strong network of people with direct interest in the success of the project.

On 17 February 2010, the co-op was given the keys to the building, and over the following 14 weeks the members worked together to refurbish the pub. However, changes to the building did not stop when the pub officially re-opened, under new tenants, in June 2010. Instead, the villagers have incrementally added functions to the property, which now features community allotments that supply the pub and shop with fresh produce, an internet café, a small library which works with the county council, and a beer garden. They also opened 'The Little Shop', which claims to be the smallest community-owned shop in the UK, located in a 3m x 3m annexe that also serves as a parcel drop-off point. The much increased range of functions has led to increased footfall at the pub, which has been good for turnover and for the viability of the venture – which, without costly mortgage commitments, is less vulnerable to outside factors than the previous owner was. Equally, the increased sense of co-ownership means that the pub is now visited much more frequently, for example as a venue for members' family events.

Almost a year after re-opening, the George and Dragon continues to be in development; there are currently plans to open a small B&B on the first floor. Almost half of the villagers have put money in the co-operative, which has had to start a waiting list for potential investors from outside.

IMPACT

The opening of the George and Dragon and the Little Shop has given the Hudswell community a revitalised social meeting place as well as their first shop in decades. With both entities dedicated to sourcing produce and products locally, the initiative has worked as a catalyst for increased local trading, leading to a strengthened local economy as well as environmental benefits, as they have reduced the number of trips to neighbouring towns.

KEY LESSONS

GENERATING CHANGE THROUGH NETWORKS

The role of external expertise

The Hudswell co-operative has been proactive in seeking advice and expertise from the very onset. It became part of the government-supported Community Shares pilot and had representatives from Co-operative and Mutual Solutions, Pub is the Hub and the Plunkett Foundation on its advisory board. They also liaised with the Development Trusts Association, Rural Action North Yorkshire, the Old Crown in Heskett Newmarket (the UK's first co-operatively owned pub) and the county and district councils throughout the process. This has enabled the co-op to develop a solid business plan, obtain investment and more easily apply for grants and funding.

RE-USING EXISTING ASSETS

Doubling up resources

The Hudswell residents have been especially innovative in their approach to rethinking and re-utilising existing community assets, even beyond the community shares approach. By incorporating the Little Shop into the existing building and making it work as an extension of the pub kitchen, the co-op was able to reduce not only rental overheads but also labour costs, as the pub staff effectively double as shopkeepers during the evenings. This allows the shop to stay open beyond the hours it is staffed by volunteers.

AN OPEN-ENDED APPROACH

Building on success

Whilst the Hudswell co-operative was originally formed to revive the George and Dragon pub, it soon developed a broader vision. The new allotments, library, internet access and the Little Shop all became part of the proposed project, and the plans to add a B&B and open-air spaces for community functions were developed in response to suggestions from local people. Such proposals are subject to the board's assessment of their potential community value, as well as the tenants' evaluation of the business proposition, thereby ensuring that the initiatives are both financially and socially sustainable.

IN CONCLUSION

How do we not just maintain but also expand the quality of service provision in villages and neighbourhoods? The takeover of the George and Dragon shows how, backed by innovative finance tools, a community can imagine, fund and run a wider range of facilities for common use. Crucially, this can only happen by devising smart combinations of functions and roles within one place – the essence of a true community hub.

OTHER EXAMPLES

Yarpole Community Shop and Post Office, Herefordshire, UK, 2004
…is a co-operative-owned enterprise that was first set up in a leased Portacabin in the backyard of a local pub; in 2009 it moved to a local church, and a gallery and café were added.

Berrynarbor Community Post Office, Berrynarbor, UK, 2004
…is a community-owned shop and post office, which is run by local residents who established a co-op to save their post office from closing.

Topsham Ales Co-operative, Devon, UK, 2010
… is a co-operative micro-brewery that operates out of the backyard of a Topsham hotel. Its first ale was produced in January 2011 and is now sold to various pubs around Exeter.

A local volunteer discusses kitchen appliances as part of the detailed household survey

09

HOUSEHOLD ENERGY SERVICES

A LOCAL ENERGY SAVINGS NETWORK
BISHOP'S CASTLE, UNITED KINGDOM

'We've got one particular volunteer, an amazing woman who set out to survey her whole street. She did a couple of people and they were really pleased, so they told some of their friends, and that soon grew to create a little community, as word about the scheme spread from home to home.'

Rachel Francis, Household Energy Services

1 IN 4	17%	£0
HOUSEHOLDS IN BISHOP'S CASTLE HAVE TAKEN SURVEY	AVERAGE CARBON EMISSION REDUCTIONS RESULTING FROM SURVEY	COST OF SURVEY TO HOUSEHOLD

GENERATING A VIRTUOUS CYCLE OF ADVICE, SAVINGS AND WORD OF MOUTH

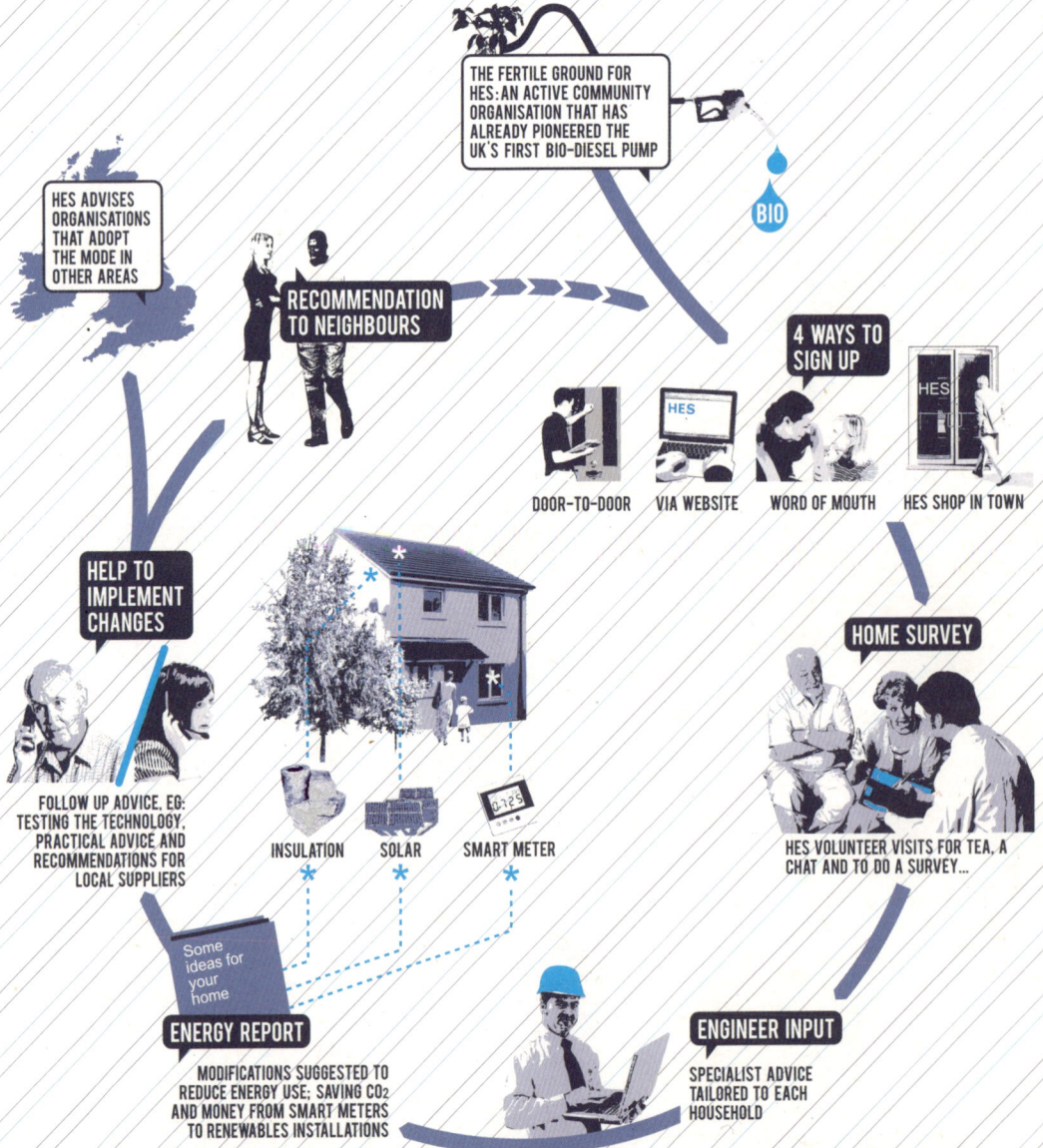

THE FERTILE GROUND FOR HES: AN ACTIVE COMMUNITY ORGANISATION THAT HAS ALREADY PIONEERED THE UK'S FIRST BIO-DIESEL PUMP

BIO

HES ADVISES ORGANISATIONS THAT ADOPT THE MODE IN OTHER AREAS

RECOMMENDATION TO NEIGHBOURS

4 WAYS TO SIGN UP

DOOR-TO-DOOR

VIA WEBSITE

WORD OF MOUTH

HES SHOP IN TOWN

HELP TO IMPLEMENT CHANGES

FOLLOW UP ADVICE, EG: TESTING THE TECHNOLOGY, PRACTICAL ADVICE AND RECOMMENDATIONS FOR LOCAL SUPPLIERS

INSULATION   SOLAR   SMART METER

HOME SURVEY

HES VOLUNTEER VISITS FOR TEA, A CHAT AND TO DO A SURVEY...

Some ideas for your home

ENERGY REPORT

MODIFICATIONS SUGGESTED TO REDUCE ENERGY USE; SAVING CO2 AND MONEY FROM SMART METERS TO RENEWABLES INSTALLATIONS

ENGINEER INPUT

SPECIALIST ADVICE TAILORED TO EACH HOUSEHOLD

THE STORY

In Bishop's Castle in Shropshire, one in four households have had a personalised energy survey done. Driven by volunteers, this initiative uses local trusted networks to generate significant household energy reductions in the town – and in the wider region.

Household Energy Services (HES) is a unique peer-to-peer advice service that has translated the complex policy challenge of climate change into a credible, low-cost pathway to everyday lifestyle adjustments. The surveys grew out of the Wasteless Society, an entrepreneurial community group active since the 1990s, which had already pioneered an anaerobic digesting project and a biodiesel pump using recycled vegetable oil. In 2004 they conducted a survey that revealed that the village's carbon footprint was well above the UK average, and that most carbon emissions resulted from the way people heated their homes and moved about. This led the society to start offering free home surveys, in order to provide people with customised advice on reducing their energy use.

To deal with the increased demand for energy surveys, the Wasteless Society set up Light Foot Enterprise, a community interest company (CIC) with a small number of paid staff. The actual surveys are carried out by volunteers, who are given six hours training and sent out to collect data on household structure, energy use and transport behaviour. This information is sent to a professional energy surveyor, who produces a tailored report with recommendations on reducing the household's energy use, through cost-free behavioural changes such as remembering to turn off the lights, or through bigger investments such as installing solar panels. The report also provides information on available grants and invites householders to contact HES for further technical advice or recommendations for trusted energy solutions providers. HES also lends out devices such as smart energy meters that people can test in their homes.

Although HES is based primarily on volunteer labour, it still has staff and maintenance costs, which have mainly been covered through grants and donations. In 2010 HES was a joint winner of NESTA's £1,000,000 Big Green Challenge prize, which has helped it to expand the initiative into a social enterprise available to other communities. In the coming years, HES plans to implement a membership scheme, in which initial surveys will remain free but members will benefit from discounts and professional advice.

IMPACT

To date, more than 1,500 HES surveys have been conducted, resulting in significant carbon emission reductions and tangible financial benefits resulting from energy savings. Savings in carbon emissions from regular household and transport activities average 17%. The scheme has spread beyond Bishop's Castle, to five other areas in Wales and England; the organisation grows by working with local environmental and community organisations that approach HES to replicate the service.

KEY LESSONS

PARTICIPATION BEYOND CONSULTATION

GENERATING CHANGE THROUGH NETWORKS

AN OPEN-ENDED APPROACH

User-led services

HES has established a no-nonsense model where local volunteers – fellow householders and energy users – give advice in layman's terms and explain how energy reduction can affect day-to-day household expenditure. Whilst the post-survey professional report includes recommendations for long-term investments, it deliberately also suggests simple behavioural changes, making it easy for all to benefit from a survey. This user-led model socialises and makes tangible a project that might otherwise be seen as difficult, intrusive, bureaucratic or profit-driven. In addition, volunteers can, if they wish, profit from an extended training programme leading to formal accreditation in what may well become a growth market.

Mass localism

The HES initiative has primarily relied on two types of networks: local volunteers who use the power of word of mouth, trusted relations and even knocking on doors; and national support organisations such as NESTA. NESTA's Big Green Challenge, a national initiative designed to stimulate and support community-led responses to climate change, provided development support and external funding, thereby enabling the project to grow to scale. In contrast, despite the initiative's evident positive impact on core policy objectives, the local authority has had no major role in HES's growth, demonstrating the need for a diversity of support pathways that can link people to resources outside their own locality.

Tackling next challenges

From their origins within the Wasteless Society to their current growth, HES and its parent company Light Foot Enterprise, have taken a practical approach to tackling environmental challenges on an incremental basis. Rather than creating an overarching strategy, the approach is based on step-by-step experimentation, collaborative data gathering and low-barrier local discussions. A next initiative, Farm Carbon, further develops the ambitions of the organisation by bringing farmers and carbon reduction experts together to make the energy use of agricultural operations more intelligible and sustainable.

IN CONCLUSION

What tangible steps can people take to save energy and carbon across a community? Household Energy Services shows that a deliberate approach to the social dynamics of behaviour change is crucial for building the civic economy. This generates meaningful shifts – with real local benefits – in a way that top-down policy and large-scale investment in new physical infrastructure alone cannot achieve.

OTHER EXAMPLES

The Green Valleys, Brecon Beacons, UK, 2008

...is a community interest company that has harnessed local expertise to develop renewable energy schemes and support communities to reduce their carbon emissions, primarily through hydro-electric power.

ONZO, London, UK, 2007

...is a for-profit company that grew out of The Hub Islington (see case study 10), which helps households to reduce their carbon emissions through in-house energy displays and smart meter systems.

Summerfield Eco Village, Birmingham, UK, 2004

...was a deprived inner-city neighbourhood where a housing association-led partnership enabled an eco retrofit and energy awareness project; residents are now ambassadors for the scheme and give advice in other neighbourhoods.

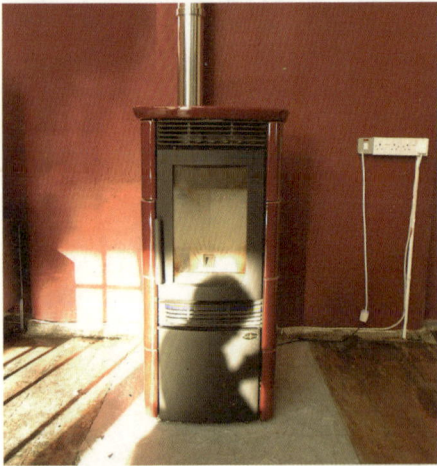

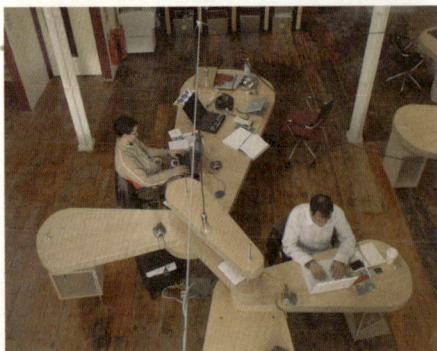

Scenes from The Hub Islington and (Bottom right) from The Hub King's Cross, the second Hub to open in London

10

THE HUB ISLINGTON

A HOME FOR CHANGE-MAKERS
LONDON, UNITED KINGDOM

'The path of any young business owes so much to the input of people you find yourself sitting next to, and at The Hub we sit next to amazing people. Before too long, people start to see what they would be capable of doing working together. Then they do it.'

Luke Nicholson, Hub member and founder of More Associates and CarbonCulture.

28
HUBS
ACROSS THE
WORLD IN 6
YEARS

72%
OF HUB ISLINGTON
MEMBERS SAY THEY
HAVE COLLABORATED
ON PROJECTS

6,000
SOCIAL PIONEERS IN
1 SOCIAL
MOVEMENT

CREATING FERTILE GROUND FOR THE SOCIAL PIONEERS OF TOMORROW

2001	2003	2005	2007	2009	2011

FUTURE HUB MEMBERS HELP CREATE & HOST THE UN ALTERNATIVE SUMMIT IN SOWETO

THE HUB FOUNDED

FIRST MEMBERS CO-DESIGN & CO-DEVELOP SPATIAL CONCEPT

FIRST HUB OPENS IN ISLINGTON

SECOND GENERATION OPENS: 6 HUBS WORLDWIDE

THIRD GENERATION OPENS: 12 HUBS WORLDWIDE

THERE ARE NOW 28 HUBS ACROSS 6 CONTINENTS

KITCHEN: THE SOCIAL HEART OF THE HUB

ENERGY USE MINIMISED THROUGH HIGH OCCUPANCY

HOT-DESKING ENCOURAGES SOCIABILITY

INTERIOR LAYOUT CO-DEVELOPED BY MEMBERS GROWS SENSE OF BELONGING

SOCIAL TABLES DESIGNED BY MEMBERS

SHARING OF IDEAS, CONCEPTS AND KNOWLEDGE HELPS START-UPS TO SUCCEED

HACKABLE INTERIOR ENCOURAGES MEMBERS TO ADAPT AND CONTRIBUTE TO THE SPACE

THE HOST: CONNECTING A COMMUNITY OF PRACTICE THROUGH DAILY INTERACTION

ETHICALLY SOURCED MATERIALS & MEMBER-BUILT LIBRARY COMMUNICATE HUB ETHOS

ADJUSTABLE & SOCIABLE FURNITURE ENCOURAGES PEER-TO-PEER INTERACTION

MEMBERSHIP TARIFF BASED ON TIME NOT SPACE ALLOWS FOR HIGH UTILISATION RATE

ADAPTABLE SPACE HELPS TRANSFORM SPACE FOR MULTIPLE FUNCTIONS / DIVERSE PROGRAMME OF USE

THE STORY

Incubating good ideas is about more than just the provision of cheap desks. From its beginnings on a warehouse floor in North London, The Hub has become a global community for social entrepreneurs, a network of 28 spaces worldwide and a model for exchanging ideas, know-how and a shared sense of purpose.

The Hub grew from a series of events organised by a group of socially engaged college graduates based in London. The first was the Soweto Mountain of Hope, a temporary community hub in the margins of the 2002 United Nations World Summit on Sustainable Development in South Africa, which was hailed by the then UN Secretary-General, Kofi Annan, as the 'real summit'. Perceiving how a widespread lack of access, scale and resources was holding back budding social pioneers, they had the ambition to create a permanent platform for these change-makers to work, meet, exchange ideas and knowledge, and communicate their ideas and ventures to the world.

Opened in 2004, The Hub Islington in London was the prototype of this home and 'sharing economy'. It built a hybrid business model that borrowed time-based tariffs from the mobile phone industry: instead of renting 'a desk', members book access to The Hub for, say, 50 or 100 hours per month. This enables more intensive use of space, ensuring financial viability as well as encouraging communication.

Crucially, The Hub was built not just as a workspace solution but a place that encourages deep affinity, co-ownership and the sense of being part of a movement – a subtle but significant shift from 'selling a space' to customers to 'giving space' for a community of practice. Collaboration on concept development, co-design and even the refitting of the warehouse space helped build this community with a shared sense of purpose. Furthermore, with a physical space purposefully designed to accommodate a wide range of events and meetings, a sociable atmosphere was established.

The Hub also depends on investments in the social process: a deliberate 'hosting' strategy was developed to facilitate knowledge exchange, and this has become a central element as The Hub has expanded far beyond Islington. Every Hub has at least one host permanently present in the space, to welcome newcomers, manage everyday business and help members connect to one another. In addition, this is increasingly complemented by active peer-to-peer learning programmes and the development of social impact investment tools.

Sophisticated design strategies for the space and its furniture maximise sociability, adaptability and diversity of working modes, whilst simultaneously communicating The Hub's social and environmental ethics, backed up through social media and online knowledge-sharing tools, and the building of a global network. This has allowed an expansion model whereby Hubs across the world can respond to local needs whilst retaining the principles and qualities of the model.

IMPACT

Across the Hub network, thousands of new ventures have been started, realised, connected with seed-funding and introduced to prospective partners and clients. Moreover, the vast majority of members say The Hub has helped to improve their work-life as social entrepreneurs and enabled them to secure sales and to collaborate with like-minded people. On average, each Hub member takes on an extra 2.5 employees within 12 months of joining. Also, the environmental cost of the space is greatly reduced by its intensive usage, with an average workspace of 4.5 sq m as opposed to the 15 sq m standard across the affordable workspace sector.

KEY LESSONS

FINANCIAL CO-INVESTMENT

A vested community

Hubs have relied on a remarkable diversity in initial investment sources. Hub founders have used volunteer time and donated materials to lower the capital cost, and devised micro-bond schemes that allow a large number of potential supporters to invest small amounts of money. This approach means many Hubs can remain independent of public sector support, with operational costs covered by membership fees. A shared characteristic of these diverse finance methods is that they rely on the building of trust within dense social networks that are motivated by The Hub's mission.

THE EXPERIENCE OF PLACE

The role of hosting

Whilst the physical architecture of a Hub is important to communicate its ethics and to set the right conditions for use, the Hub model goes beyond physical space. The hosts are a crucial part of the community that The Hub seeks to create: they facilitate a shared knowledge infrastructure by actively connecting members to other entrepreneurs, helping to link up emerging ideas, and facilitating peer-to-peer support and access to additional investment. They also manage the place and organise events in a way that maintains a strong shared ethos, thus creating the fertile ground for innovation and collaboration.

GENERATING CHANGE THROUGH NETWORKS

Local adoption and adaptation

Entrepreneurs across the world can adopt and adapt the Hub model with practical support from a core Hub team. Certain elements, such as the mission, key components of the space and the 'hosting' model, are a part of the shared concept but the kind of space, local network and focus of activities can vary significantly in response to local conditions. Whilst this has enabled a rapid growth of the Hub model, the challenge is to generate the resources to support this process and create a strong shared network of know-how and experience.

IN CONCLUSION

How do we grow the fertile ground for the next generation of change-makers? This is about more than the careful design of space alone: it is about hosting open networks and building peer-to-peer communities of practice. Initiatives such as The Hub, enabled by innovative finance and co-investment, can ignite and speed up the new social ventures that are crucial to the civic economy. They form the type of business infrastructure needed for a re-balanced local economy.

OTHER EXAMPLES

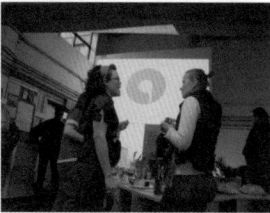

OpenSpace, Manchester, UK, 2008
...is a co-operative co-working project that offers cheap, flexible office space for freelancers, ethical businesses and social enterprises in an open work environment that facilitates interaction and collaboration.

Hub Culture, worldwide, 2002
...is a social network service (unrelated to The Hub) that has set up permanent and temporary membership-based workspaces in 15 cities, offering a variety of professional services and flexible meeting spaces.

Centre for Social Innovation, Toronto, Canada, 2003
...is a social enterprise pioneering collaborative workspaces in the city, inspired by the open-source movement, which offers flexible, shared spaces for social innovators.

Children play ball in their yard next to the Hørsholm plant

11

HØRSHOLM WASTE-TO-ENERGY

A NEIGHBOURHOOD CLEAN-TECH INCINERATOR
HØRSHOLM, DENMARK

'Living next-door to a waste incinerator was never a problem for us. It was clean and silent, and, to be honest, we hardly ever noticed it. Except, of course, when the heating bill arrived.'

Camilla Reimann, former Hørsholm resident

93% WASTE DIVERTED FROM LANDFILLS

60% RECYCLED

33% INCINERATED

80% LOCAL HEAT GENERATED FOR 10,000 HOMES THROUGH WASTE - TO - ENERGY PLANT & NETWORK

30% CHEAPER HEATING BILLS

RE-IMAGINING A WASTE INSTALLATION AS LOCAL CIVIC INFRASTRUCTURE

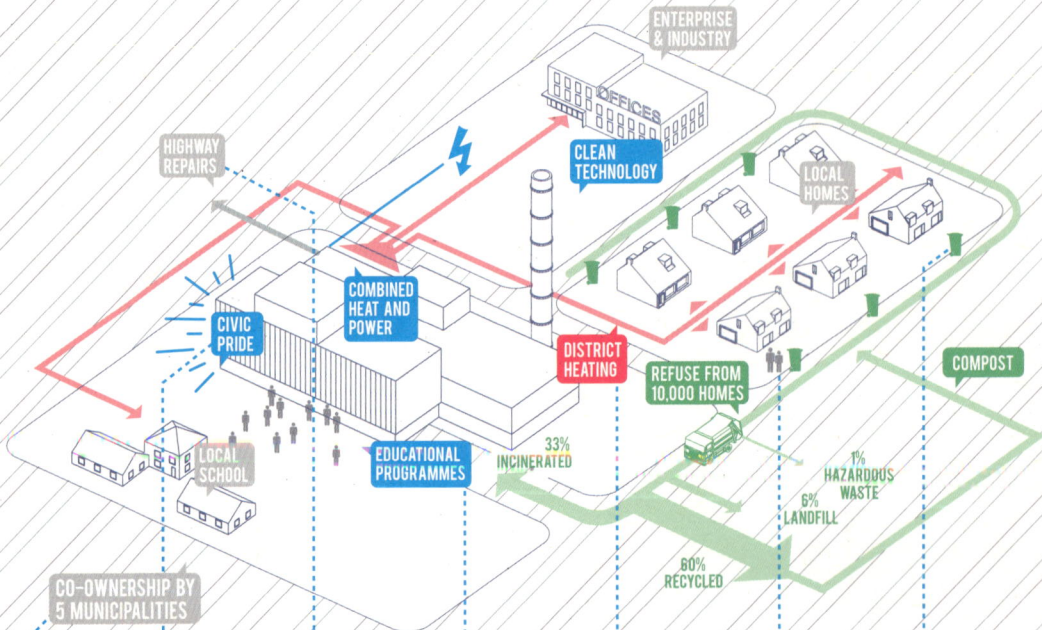

ENTERPRISE & INDUSTRY

OFFICES

CLEAN TECHNOLOGY

LOCAL HOMES

HIGHWAY REPAIRS

COMBINED HEAT AND POWER

CIVIC PRIDE

DISTRICT HEATING

REFUSE FROM 10,000 HOMES

COMPOST

LOCAL SCHOOL

EDUCATIONAL PROGRAMMES

33% INCINERATED

1% HAZARDOUS WASTE

6% LANDFILL

60% RECYCLED

CO-OWNERSHIP BY 5 MUNICIPALITIES

CO-GOVERNANCE: 5 ELECTED MAYORS MAINTAIN ACTIVE ROLE ON BOARD OF DIRECTORS

GOOD DESIGN: ARCHITECTURE USED TO COMMUNICATE THE INTERNAL PROCESS & FOSTER CIVIC PRIDE

CLOSING THE LOOP: ELECTRICITY FOR LOCAL COMMUNITY AND MATERIAL FOR MAINTAINING ROADS

AWARENESS: EDUCATIONAL AND OTHER OUTREACH PROGRAMMES MAINTAIN PUBLIC AWARENESS & TRUST

FINANCIAL REWARD: HEATING BILLS REDUCED BY UP TO 30%, RAISING HOUSE VALUES

SHARED MENTALITY: PLANT SEEN AS BENEFICIAL RATHER THAN SIMPLY AN INFRASTRUCTURAL NECESSITY

TANGIBLE GAIN: ORGANIC WASTE COMPOSTED AND DISTRIBUTED TO HOUSEHOLDS AS FERTILISER

THE STORY

Each year, the UK sends 350 million tons of waste to landfill. This equals five tons per capita and represents a significant cost to taxpayers. With recent EU legislation prohibiting the creation of new landfills, other options for waste processing will be required, but incineration, one of the most obvious alternatives, has attracted widespread opposition in Britain. In one Danish town, however, a more positive approach has turned waste into a resource.

In Hørsholm, collaboration between local authorities, business and the community has meant that non-recyclable materials that might otherwise be sent to landfill are being treated at an incinerator in the very heart of the town. The inter-municipal waste management company, Nordforbrænding, receives all the household and industrial waste in the five municipalities that co-own it. Its incinerator waste-to-energy plant then generates electricity and heats 10,000 homes through a district heating system, reducing the residents' heating bills by 30%.

Since Nordforbrænding was established in 1969, it has increasingly focused on efficient use of the heat the incinerator generates. Encouraged in particular by the energy crises of the 1970s, a combined heat and power system was established as the plant expanded. Residents actively support and trust its presence because they see it not as an unavoidable utility provider, but as a community not-for-profit asset that generates direct local benefits – homes connected to the district heating system tend to have a higher value because of the energy cost savings generated through the plant. An important precondition for this was the obligation on Nordforbrænding to use the best available technology, which has minimised nuisance in relation to smell, smoke and noise and allowed it to maintain high levels of trust.

Particular attention was also paid to the plant's architecture, so that it could be embedded in a residential neighbourhood. Instead of aiming to 'hide' the facility in an industrial estate, this civic infrastructure has been designed to be an object of civic pride.

In 1997, Denmark became the first country in Europe to make it illegal to take waste suitable for incineration to landfills. Today, there are 29 waste-to-energy plants across the country, 21 of which are co-owned by adjacent local authorities, with the others belonging to private energy companies; 10 more incinerators are in the pipeline. Many plants have, like Hørsholm, opted to create landmark pieces of architecture, often incorporating large areas of glass to convey transparency and designed by leading international architects.

Throughout Denmark there is a shared public awareness of the need to deal with waste responsibly. In addition to waste incineration, Nordforbrænding is engaged in managing recycling stations, collecting hazardous waste, managing a landfill and facilitating collaboration on waste reduction in the participating municipalities. In this respect, the Hørsholm plant is more than just a single facility, as it is part of an integrated local waste and energy management system. A local dimension to this – that is, the siting of facilities in or near the neighbourhoods they serve – is inevitable, and the way in which the particular benefits of waste-to-energy have been realised and communicated has been integral to ensuring this is locally accepted and welcomed.

IMPACT

Hørsholm now sends only special categories of waste (less than 6% of the total) to landfill: 60% is recycled, 33% incinerated and 1% is hazardous waste that goes for special treatment. The local waste-to-energy plant generates 80% of Hørsholm's heat and 20% of its electricity. People living close to an incinerator generally enjoy heating bills 30% lower than the national average. Several waste-to-energy plants are currently being planned, and many municipalities across the country are working on extending the existing district heating grid to connect even more households to this cheap heating source. Together with high recycling rates, this process significantly benefits carbon reduction by substituting for fossil energy sources. Moreover, the landfill charge to Denmark's households is amongst the lowest in the EU.

KEY LESSONS

PARTICIPATION BEYOND CONSULTATION

Sharing the benefits

The success of the Hørsholm waste-to-energy plant can be largely attributed to the direct benefits that local residents see in the form of tangible electricity and heating bill savings. This creates a high degree of community co-ownership over what is technically 'just' a public-private clean-tech infrastructure. The Hørsholm incinerator is connected with the community through its physical infrastructure and through its governance: the mayors of the five participating municipalities form the board of directors.

RE-USING EXISTING ASSETS

Waste as resource

Fundamentally, the Hørsholm approach recognises waste as an asset. This improves the status of waste-handling facilities – rather than this being a 'locally unwanted land use' it is instead regarded as a productive civic infrastructure that can be integrated in the everyday fabric of neighbourhoods. This is communicated through the physical design and aesthetics of the plant, as visual manifestation of a trusted system.

RECOGNISING WHERE VALUE LIES

Maintaining trust

Whilst in Denmark there has long been a high level of trust in waste incineration, local factors such as governance and community benefits are crucial in maintaining it. Nordforbrænding also works actively to engage schools, organisations and individuals through education – for example, free tours customised to suit individual needs are offered to anyone interested. By understanding the entirety of the waste cycle, people gain a stronger sense of responsibility, thereby engendering a commitment to waste-to-energy as part of the process. After all, in the long run this model is only sustainable if it is understood and trusted.

IN CONCLUSION

How do we make it desirable to build the local utility infrastructure that we need? Local utilities will be welcome in people's back yard if we imagine, build, govern and communicate them as vital elements of local neighbourhoods that generate direct and tangible benefits to people – lowering the cost of living and making places more resilient in the face of environmental change.

OTHER EXAMPLES

Richmond Hill Energy-from-Waste Plant, Isle of Man, 2004
...is a strikingly designed facility owned by the private waste management company SITA, which produces 10% of the island's electricity by processing all its waste.

Islington Business Waste Recycling Project, London, UK, 2009
...was an award-winning project by the Islington Chamber of Commerce to increase recycling and reuse rates by offering free, independent assistance to businesses and third sector organisations in the borough; its services have since been mainstreamed.

Torrs Hydro, New Mills, UK, 2008
...is a community-owned and funded hydropower scheme, the profits from which are reinvested into the community.

Tending the strawberries and other plants growing in a mini-garden made from an old dinghy in the Todmorden High School grounds

12

INCREDIBLE EDIBLE TODMORDEN

A MOVEMENT GROWN IN PUBLIC SPACE
TODMORDEN, UNITED KINGDOM

'You just need to understand how we all tick. And we're all the same. We're bored to death and cynical about strategies and policies and rhetoric. But what we like is action, we like to get involved in things and we like things to point at.'

Pam Warhurst, co-founder, Incredible Edible Todmorden

600
FRUIT TREES
PLANTED **1** PER
2.5 RESIDENTS

40
GROWING SITES
IN THE TOWN
CENTRE

33%
RESIDENTS TAKE
PART IN IET
ACTIVITIES

BUILDING A SHARED LANGUAGE AROUND BEHAVIOUR CHANGE

AN OPEN INVITATION TO THE WIDER COMMUNITY

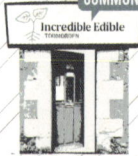

A COALITION OF LIKE-MINDED COMMUNITY LEADERS

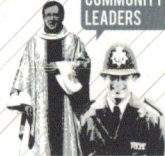

TELLING STORIES THROUGH ORGANISED EVENTS

'OPEN DOOR' COMMUNITY PRESENCE AS CAFE = LOW BARRIER TO ENTRY

PARTNERSHIPS WITH LOCAL GROUPS (POLICE, SCHOOLS ETC) OPEN UP SPACES & SUPPORT

EVENTS ORGANISING- SOCIALISING THE ACTIVITY

SEEDING THE MOVEMENT

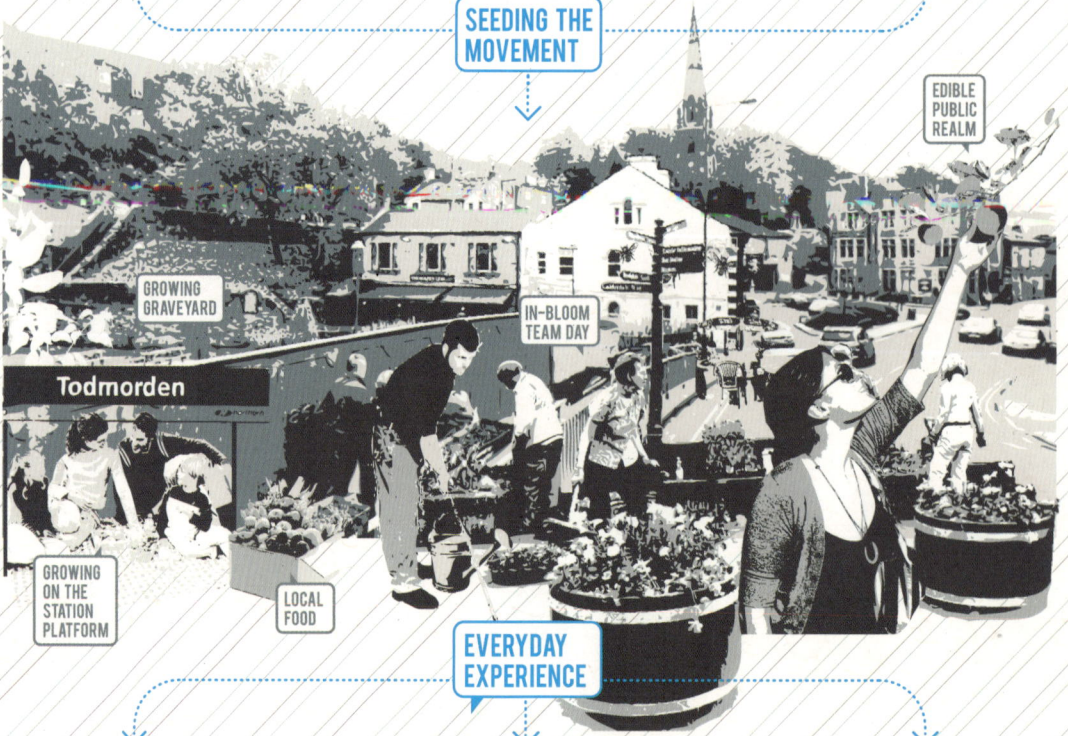

EDIBLE PUBLIC REALM

GROWING GRAVEYARD

IN-BLOOM TEAM DAY

Todmorden

GROWING ON THE STATION PLATFORM

LOCAL FOOD

EVERYDAY EXPERIENCE

EDIBLE PLANTING AVAILABLE TO THE GENERAL PUBLIC

STRONG COMMUNITY PRIDE AND CO-WORKING TO MAINTAIN & NURTURE GREEN SPACES

NEW USES AND APPRECIATION FOR EXISTING SPACES

THE STORY

Imagine waiting at the train station for your commute home, feeling peckish, and simply grabbing a piece of fruit from a tree right off the side of the platform. Implausible? Not in the Lancashire town of Todmorden. For nearly three years the town's residents, young and old, have been busy taking over car parks, grass verges, graveyards, pavements and schoolyards and turning them into edible landscapes. Few places have made the shift to a local food system more tangible and enjoyable.

The efforts are led by a loose coalition of residents who have challenged established notions of what physical changes people can create in the public realm. After an initial 'guerrilla-gardening' appropriation of open spaces for food growing, the initiators started approaching both public sector and private landowners for permission to plant on their underused grounds. Examples include Northern Rail, the fire and police stations, the local social housing landlord and a church that has allowed crops to be planted on the graveyard. Since 2009, Incredible Edible Todmorden (IET) has worked with Calderdale Council to make it easier for individuals and groups to plant on council-owned land. In a step with both symbolic and practical value, the council reduced the licence processing fee from £107 to £10 and smoothed other procedures. However, IET does not aim to obtain public funding for its regular planting activities, looking only for collaboration.

No formal membership is required to start growing, but Todmorden residents are encouraged to farm wherever and whenever they can. All the town's schools and several public and private bodies are engaged in the campaign. Schools now grow food in raised beds and polytunnels and involve students in the harvesting

and preparation of produce. The local health centre has started an 'apothecary garden', and one housing association has launched its own Edible Pennine initiative, offering tenants a free starter pack with seeds and advice.

The scheme is a virtuous cycle: the improvements in the physical environment make residents proud of their town, which in turn has generated further support for resident-led public realm initiatives. The market for locally produced food has grown, and Nimbyism has been reduced, as the scheme's benefits are both tangible and collectively owned. There have been no incidents of garden vandalism, and raised beds adjacent to pubs have been astonishingly free of cigarette butts and glass shards.

However, the mission of Incredible Edible Todmorden goes beyond public space alone; rather, the highly visible public realm activities are a way of getting a greater number of people engaged in changing their daily behaviours, in order to grow a movement to build a more sustainable local economy. The organisation therefore also advocates local food production and consumption through initiatives such as the 'Every Egg Matters' campaign, food festivals and communal beekeeping. In addition, it has secured funding for a Food Hub, which will also serve as an educational centre.

IMPACT

The number of food growing sites within Todmorden town centre is increasing; more than 600 fruit trees have been planted, and the IET 'Egg Map' identifies 50 local egg producers. Six Incredible Edible campaigns have been launched in other towns and Granada in Spain became the first Incredible Edible town beyond the UK. As a consequence of the increased tourism its campaign has generated, IET has been able to hire two paid part-time 'food inspirers' as educators and tourist guides. Beyond this, the IET campaign has also generated a shared sense of pride and enthusiasm in Todmorden, connecting diverse people to a long-term movement through the common language of food.

KEY LESSONS

RECOGNISING THE PROTAGONISTS

The storytellers

A core group of initiators started by planting 'propaganda gardens' on prominent sites in the town centre, relying on what they themselves call 'storytelling' to generate awareness, support and behaviour shifts amongst local people. Their narrative about the problems of the global food system and its environmental and health impact underpinned all their initial efforts – and has been made accessible and welcoming through the practical approach taken. This twin strategy – direct action and communicating purpose – created a wider social network and generated access to the media and local authorities.

PARTICIPATION BEYOND CONSULTATION

An open invitation

IET encourages anyone to plant at any time and place, and to participate in whichever manner they want. It invites people to be part of a movement without the trappings of becoming part of an organisation, thus growing change through a groundswell of initiatives instead of a top-down strategy. IET does help people become more skilled at planting and tending crops, enabling wider participation. This action-led approach has meant IET needed little external financial support to become successful. Formal strategic planning responded to the initiative instead of driving it: in response to widely acknowledged success, local licensing rules were changed to lower a barrier for participation.

RE-USING EXISTING ASSETS

Bringing public space back to life

Fundamentally, the IET project recognises that many public spaces or spaces owned by service providers are underutilised, and that local people can improve them through relatively small interventions. The scheme is low-cost, as it is based on the exploitation of derelict land, and most community gardens have been built using recycled materials.

IN CONCLUSION

How to interpret the 'public' in public realm in a way that activates people to co-produce the spaces they use every day? Incredible Edible Todmorden shows what happens if we open up the public domain to the smallest scale of investment. Crucially, starting with visible, low-threshold interventions builds a shared language of change as a pathway for future steps – the fertile ground we need for wider behaviour change, new civic entrepreneurialism and participative citizenship.

OTHER EXAMPLES

Middlesbrough Town Meal, Middlesbrough, UK, 2006
...is a free annual event where local residents gather in public spaces to experience home-grown and home-cooked food provided by local growing communities and individuals.

Nomadisch Grün, Berlin, Germany, 2009
...is a 'nomadic' gardening project that temporarily transforms unused spaces such as building sites, car parks and warehouse roofs into urban farmland and green meeting places.

Growing Communities, London, UK, 1993
...is a social enterprise that harnesses collective buying power to link communities straight to small-scale sustainable farms around London via a fruit-and-veg box scheme and a local farmers market, as well as producing food at a series of organic market gardens.

The Jayride integrated mobile sharing platform

13

JAYRIDE

A PEER-TO-PEER RIDE SHARING WEBSITE
NEW ZEALAND

'I am driving back to my home state to see my parents for Christmas. Anyone who has an interesting story to tell can come along free of charge (it's a long way). I have a crappy small car, but it does the job.'

User advertisement on Jayride, 22 December 2010

5,000
MEMBERS

80,000
RIDES SHARED SINCE 2007

9,000
AVERAGE NUMBER
OF RIDES AVAILABLE
ONLINE

UNLOCKING SHARED ACCESS TO THE RESOURCES WE ALREADY HAVE

2001

GERMAN "MITFAHRGE-LEGENHEIT" WEBSITE LAUNCHES

2007

FOUNDER INSPIRED BY GERMAN PRECEDENT; CREATES HITCH.CO.NZ

2008

DEMAND OUTSTRIPS HITCH WEBSITE CAPACITY

WEBSITE RE-LAUNCHED AS JAYRIDE

JAYRIDE FOUNDERS EMBARK ON PROMOTIONAL TOUR ACROSS NEW ZEALAND; SITE & BLOG GAIN LOCAL MEDIA ATTENTION

2010

JAYRIDE AUSTRALIA LAUNCHES

2011

5,000 MEMBERS ACROSS THE COUNTRY

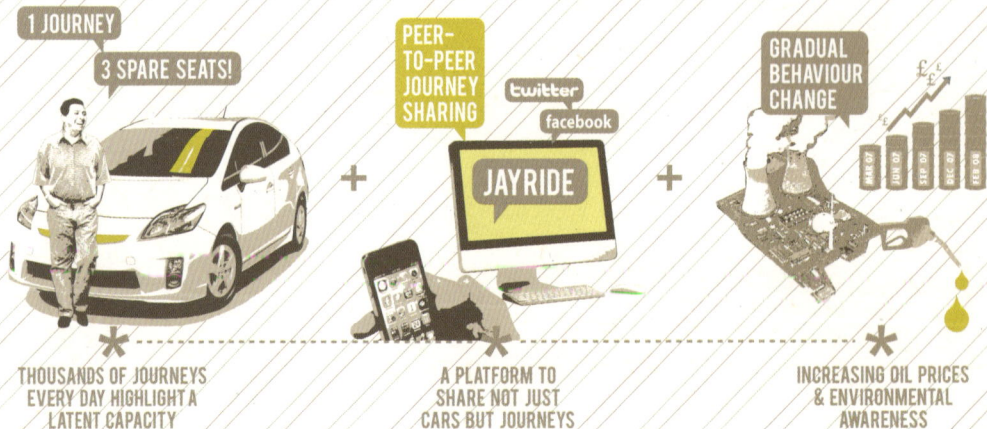

1 JOURNEY

3 SPARE SEATS!

PEER-TO-PEER JOURNEY SHARING · twitter · facebook · JAYRIDE

GRADUAL BEHAVIOUR CHANGE

* THOUSANDS OF JOURNEYS EVERY DAY HIGHLIGHT A LATENT CAPACITY

* A PLATFORM TO SHARE NOT JUST CARS BUT JOURNEYS

* INCREASING OIL PRICES & ENVIRONMENTAL AWARENESS

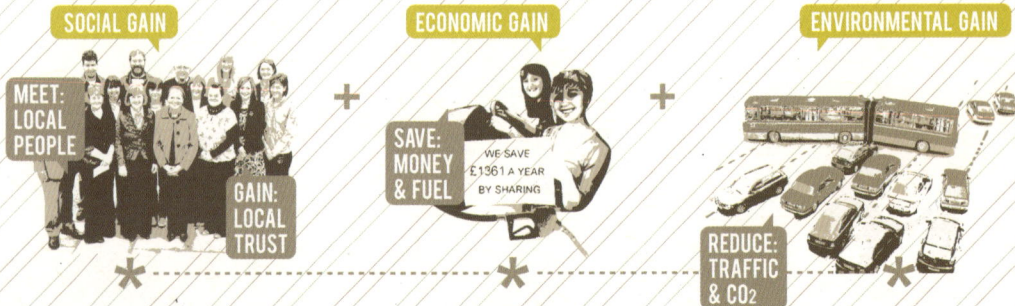

SOCIAL GAIN

MEET: LOCAL PEOPLE

GAIN: LOCAL TRUST

ECONOMIC GAIN

SAVE: MONEY & FUEL

WE SAVE £1361 A YEAR BY SHARING

ENVIRONMENTAL GAIN

REDUCE: TRAFFIC & CO_2

THE STORY

Among the many car and bicycle sharing schemes that are cropping up globally, Jayride stands out as a genuine peer-to-peer model. Unlike most hire schemes, which offer their own fleets of cars or bikes, Jayride focuses on making better use of existing resources: the cars that people already own.

Taking inspiration from a similar model in Germany, Auckland entrepreneur Rod Bishop created hitch.co.nz in 2007. It quickly became New Zealand's biggest ride-sharing website, and within two years, demand vastly outstripped the simple website's capacity. Bishop teamed up with Ross Lin, a senior developer for an online trading site, and together, they revamped and re-launched the website as Jayride in 2008.

The new web platform facilitates the sharing of rides either on a one-off or a regular basis. While each car in a conventional car share replaces an average of four to eight vehicles, Jayride further reduces the number of car miles travelled, by enabling multiple users to share the same trip, and helps people save money on fuel.

The website has a simple and easily comprehensible interface based on Google Maps, which offers a quick overview of available rides at various rates. The individuals or companies with cars have the flexibility to set a charge or offer the ride for free; they can even set a price and keep the profits themselves, thus offering car owners an additional income from assets they already have. Jayride itself makes no charges for usage – its income comes from advertising.

User profiles and feedback systems encourage trust between individuals, overcoming an obstacle often seen to have impeded large-scale car-pooling. The appeal of Jayride is further enhanced by how it generates awareness of ride-sharing as a social activity; when the website was re-launched in 2008, for example, the founders travelled across New Zealand purely through ride sharing, and blogged about their experiences.

IMPACT

By April 2011 Jayride had more than 5,000 members who have shared more than 80,000 rides, and is expanding abroad. The scheme's contribution to New Zealand's current transport and environmental challenges is increasingly being acknowledged by local authorities across the country. In particular, it is credited with integrating the existing phenomenon of ride sharing with social media, thereby increasing its appeal and convenience.

KEY LESSONS

PARTICIPATION BEYOND CONSULTATION

A platform for co-production

Jayride uses a simple web interface that is easy to navigate. This lowers barriers to participation in terms of technological capability and allows a wide range of people to use the scheme. The website facilitates the creation of personal relationships crucial to peer-to-peer services and allows users to barter and negotiate rides on their own terms. By addressing the space between mass collectivism and individuals' wishes for convenience and flexibility, Jayride provides a small-scale but growing alternative to mainstream public and private sector transport solutions.

GENERATING CHANGE THROUGH NETWORKS

Expansion through adoption

Jayride is expanding abroad, to Australia, the UK and Ireland. As a generic platform, the same infrastructure can facilitate local interactions worldwide, allowing the model to be easily scaled up beyond its original geographical boundaries, while still being highly tailored to local populations and relying on local social networks. Beyond its main website, Jayride also takes advantage of social media platforms such as Facebook and Twitter. By featuring interesting rides or impulsive last-minute vacation plans on these sites, Jayride succeeds in building interest around the company as more than just a utilitarian service: sharing rides is presented as an appealing social experience as well as a practical option.

RE-USING EXISTING ASSETS

Use not ownership

Jayride is part of a growing trend that sees resources for daily use – whether a workplace or a means of transport – not as question of ownership or fixed rental agreement but as a challenge of organising highly flexible access. In this case both the user and the provider consist of the public at large; the role of the platform infrastructure is that it solves two market failures, namely lack of information and the absence of a contractual base for strangers to agree on shared occasional or repeated use. As such, despite being a very light-touch and low-cost sharing software, it fundamentally enables the reorganisation of a shared good – mobility – which plays a huge role in many people's quality of daily life.

IN CONCLUSION

What are the smart sustainable transport infrastructures that help us move away from 'building more' and 'buying more'? Unlocking and sharing the resources we already have is a crucial dimension – with an increase in access instead of ownership as the key objective. Jayride is one amongst many examples that show how by using new social web applications we can manage demand, save resources and build not just a new transport paradigm but also a new understanding of shared wealth.

OTHER EXAMPLES

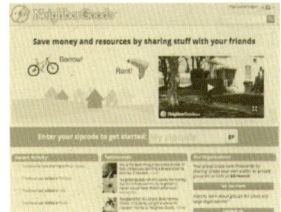

RelayRides, Boston, USA, 2010
...is a pioneering neighbour-to-neighbour car sharing service that provides insurance and technology to enable people to lend their private vehicles.

Airbnb, worldwide, 2008
...is a San Francisco-based online platform that connects people who have rooms to spare with people who are looking for a place to stay. Like Jayride, users negotiate the rents between themselves.

NeighborGoods, USA, 2010
...is an online platform that facilitates free peer-to-peer lending, borrowing and renting of all types of items.

Young people prepare the next issue of Livity's Live magazine

14

LIVITY

A YOUNG PEOPLE'S HANG-OUT AND COMMUNICATIONS AGENCY
LONDON, UNITED KINGDOM

'A friend of mine told me he was working for Live and that he was interviewing famous people like Trey Songz and I wanted that too, so I went along, met with Chantelle Fiddy, who was a mentor there at the time, and then I started working on the magazine. What's brilliant is that for everyone there's someone you click with here, because there's such a diversity of people and characters and opportunity and experiences – and that helps you find out what you want to do and what you are best at.'

Sian Anderson, 20, now a freelance PR writer for musicians including DJ Swerve and Ed Sheeran, a consultant for Livity and Island Records, and a DJ on Rinse FM; she started working on Live magazine at 15.

1,000
YOUNG PEOPLE
PER YEAR
CONTRIBUTE TO
LIVE MAGAZINE

100
YOUNG PEOPLE NOT IN
EDUCATION, EMPLOYMENT
OR TRAINING HELPED
INTO WORK EACH YEAR

6,075,456
VIEWS OF THE WORLD'S
FIRST INTERACTIVE DRAMA
SERIES SPONSORED BY
CHILDLINE

BUILDING ON THE PASSION OF YOUNG PEOPLE

2001 — **2004** — **2005** — **2007** — **2011**

LIVITY FOUNDED

FIRST CLIENTS: 02, TEENAGE CANCER TRUST, AND LAMBETH COUNCIL

LIVE MAGAZINE BECOMES STAND-ALONE SOCIAL ENTERPRISE

DUBPLATE DRAMA LAUNCHES: AN INTERACTIVE MULTI-PLATFORM DRAMA SERIES, NOW AN INTERNATIONAL FRANCHISE

MUSIC4GOOD LAUNCHES AS APPRENTICE-SHIP SCHEME FOR THE MUSIC INDUSTRY COLLABORATING WITH SONY MUSIC

SPINEBREAKERS, THE FIRST ONLINE BOOK COMMUNITY FOR TEENAGERS, LAUNCHED WITH PENGUIN BOOKS

CO-FOUNDER APPOINTED SOCIAL ENTERPRISE AMBASSADOR BY CABINET OFFICE

YOUNG PEOPLE CAN COME & GO AS THEY WANT

YOUNG PEOPLE CO-DEVELOP CAMPAIGNS, PRODUCTS AND COMMUNICATIONS MATERIAL

MENTOR ROLE SHARED BETWEEN FULL-TIME MENTORS AND OTHER LIVITY STAFF

YOUNG PEOPLE MOSTLY LEARN ABOUT LIVITY THROUGH LIVE MAGAZINE DISTRIBUTION

OFFICE LAYOUT ENCOURAGES INTERACTION BETWEEN LIVITY STAFF AND YOUNG PEOPLE WORKING ON LIVE MAGAZINE

YOUNG PEOPLE ARE INVOLVED IN WRITING, PHOTOGRAPHY, FILM-MAKING, EVENTS AND AUDIO-VISUAL PRODUCTION

CLIENT MAINSTREAM MARKETING BUDGETS USED TO FUND SOCIAL OUTCOMES FOR YOUNG PEOPLE

* CAMPAIGNS GENERATE POSITIVE BEHAVIOUR CHANGE

* YOUNG PEOPLE LEARN ABOUT WIDE VARIETY OF PROFESSIONAL ROLES AND ENTREPRENEURIAL OPPORTUNITIES

* SKILLS AND CONFIDENCE IMPROVED THROUGH DAILY PEER-TO-PEER WORKFLOOR INTERACTION

* YOUNG PEOPLE APPROACHED THROUGH THEIR STRENGTHS NOT JUST THEIR NEEDS

* SOCIAL VALUE VENTURES LAUNCHED TO BENEFIT YOUNG PEOPLE

* PERCEPTION CHANGE AMONGST LARGE COMPANIES ABOUT YOUNG PEOPLE

* YOUNG PEOPLE DO SUPPORTED PLACEMENTS WITHIN PARTNER COMPANIES

THE STORY

One of the most popular hang-outs for 12-to-21-year-olds in Brixton is, of all things, a communications agency. At Livity, they can get involved in a highly professional magazine and in a wide range of marketing and awareness campaigns. With its open-door policy and collaborative work and mentoring approach, Livity has found a way to build skills and confidence and transformed life opportunities for a large range of young people in Lambeth and beyond.

Sam Conniff and Michelle Clothier started Livity in 2001 with the intention of transforming their commercial and marketing experience into a force for good. Realising that 'brands' and 'marketing' had enduring appeal but also an increasingly bad name, they decided to see if it were possible to marry business and social responsibility through a different type of campaigning. In particular, they hoped to persuade their clients that CSR budgets were not the only way for companies to show wider commitment.

Livity's formula was simple: instead of using focus groups and surveys to find out what made the under-21s tick, the agency would invite them into its everyday office environment. This would give Livity a unique insight into youth culture, whilst the young people who dropped into the office would be rewarded through engagement with a wide range of professional activities, practical skills training, and mentoring.

At first the proposition was not easy to sell to corporates, but Livity's insistence on working on mainstream campaigns, funded from marketing budgets rather than CSR budgets, has paid off. Collaborative campaigns with Penguin books to persuade young people to read more (through launching the first online teenage book community, Spinebreakers), and an in-house apprenticeship programme for ex-offenders at Google show that such new partnership types are feasible within big businesses.

The other crucial sell was to the young people themselves. Fortunately, one of Livity's first clients was Lambeth Council, which wanted to improve its communications and outreach to young people. Livity began by inviting four members of a local youth centre into the office to work on the concept. This resulted in the publication of Live, a free magazine handed out on the streets of Brixton and elsewhere in the borough. Young people started to phone in to see if they could take part; many just showed up at the agency's door. No one was ever turned away. It was noticeable that around this time the graffiti on Livity's town centre office premises reduced considerably.

Helped by the open and supportive attitude from Lambeth Council, Live magazine would soon take on a life of its own, growing far beyond a small 'community' youth magazine into a professional venture; over the course of a year as many as 1,000 young people contribute to it – on many days there are more than 30 of them in Livity's office, easily outnumbering paid staff. Live has now grown far beyond Lambeth; it was integrated with its Home Office sponsored spin-off, Live East, and is increasingly independent from public sector funding through advertising income. Despite this scale increase, Livity is focused on maintaining the core benefits of the Livity formula: having young people – including ex-offenders and 'neets' – in the heart of the office, interacting with clients, and changing perceptions and beliefs on both sides on an everyday basis.

Also, Livity is reflecting on its business model and how it serves its objectives: it is currently a for-profit company that redirects 25% of its profits via an independent trust into bursaries and grants to help disadvantaged young people find employment. In the future, Livity hopes to bring everything under the umbrella of a single social enterprise, with an equal emphasis on the social and economic targets at the core of the business.

IMPACT

Livity can point to definite success amongst the young people who turn up regularly – over 100 of them in the last year alone have found work, some in the media industry, as film producers, writers and journalists. Thus Livity and Live contribute to Lambeth's objectives for training, employment and enterprise, as well as for engagement. Meanwhile, success on the ground attests to the impact of Livity's approach. For example, a campaign for the National Blood Service featuring singer Sabrina Washington led to a marked increase in young blood donors from a BME background.

KEY LESSONS

PARTICIPATION BEYOND CONSULTATION

The office floor as leveller

The key to Livity's success is that it provides an open door to young people – not just to hang out but to actively participate in the daily routine of Livity's campaigns and projects. They are at the heart of Live magazine and work closely with the staff producing new ideas, approaches and products – in areas from concept development to graphic design and market research. This co-creation approach means they are treated – and also actively mentored – as professionals and equals on the work floor, building self-esteem, purpose and skills through active doing not teaching. Though this can make the office a hectic place, it also gives it a crucial dynamism and feeling of involvement.

AN OPEN-ENDED APPROACH

A platform for civic start-ups

From its solid core ethos and activities, Livity has become an open platform for new ventures. In addition to Live, it has generated a music business apprenticeship scheme, Music4Good, and some-whereto, a project that offers 16-to-25-year-olds access to spaces for activities they are passionate about within the arts, culture and sports. The emphasis on face-to-face interaction in the office means that Livity itself may not easily grow beyond the 20-odd paid staff in its Brixton premises but such start-ups could spin out or be adapted by partners elsewhere. The experience with Live East, whose Whitechapel offices had to close after core funding was withdrawn and the two magazines merged, shows that this can be difficult – especially because the everyday office culture at the Brixton office is crucial to the concept.

RECOGNISING WHERE VALUE LIES

Communicating social impact

Livity has invested heavily in its mentoring programme, with a full-time careers adviser, pastoral mentor and mentorship roles across all other staff. Though the agency's success has been widely recognised both in news stories and in awards – and is evident in the stories of its young people finding good jobs and starting up their own ventures – Livity is aware of the need to be even more explicit about the social benefit it creates. It is therefore developing what it calls 'Kidflow' – a way of accounting more precisely for the number of young people they reach and what impacts they have, including the small and subtle positive stories that occur daily in the office, but are hard to record in numbers.

IN CONCLUSION

How do we build new ways of working with those young people who are hard to reach or not in education, employment or training? Livity shows that if we want to change widely held negative perceptions – amongst companies and the public and also amongst young people themselves – we need to invite them into the heart of our workplaces and see these as platforms for widening horizons and youth entrepreneurship.

OTHER EXAMPLES

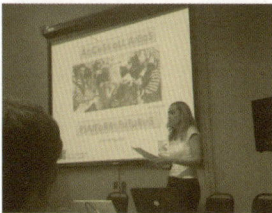

Knowle West Media Centre, Bristol, UK, 2002
...grew out of an arts and health photography project in an area that is vibrant but suffers from deprivation; a social enterprise, KWMC produces and supports high-quality media arts, working in particular with local young people.

Castlemilk Youth Complex, Glasgow, UK, 1994
...is an independent organisation founded and governed by young people from the area, which uses arts and media as a platform to provide a range of skills and personal development services and opportunities.

10thousandgirl, Australia, 2010
...is a campaign and social business that aims to improve the financial literacy of young Australian women through fun and accessible life planning and personal finance programmes; it is also creating a micro-finance fund to help women across the globe start their own business.

Traveller Ivy Buckley makes wooden flowers at Museum of East Anglian Life's yearly Gypsy arts festival

15

MUSEUM OF EAST ANGLIAN LIFE

A MUSEUM TURNED SOCIAL ENTERPRISE
STOWMARKET, UNITED KINGDOM

'I didn't say, in 2005, that we were going to become a social enterprise. It just evolved in that way. We now see the museum as the village green, intrinsically linked to the social calendar of the town. It's a place where you do business, where you meet people, where you welcome strangers, all those things. It is about opening people's eyes to the whole tapestry of life in the community.'

Tony Butler, Director, Museum of East Anglian Life

50,000
VOLUNTEER HOURS / YEAR
3.5 HOURS / RESIDENT

150 PEOPLE PROVIDED WITH ACCREDITED TRAINING SINCE 2006

40 PEOPLE HELPED INTO FULL-TIME WORK SINCE 2006

30% INCREASE IN VISITOR NUMBERS

OPENING UP A LOCAL MUSEUM AS PUBLIC SPACE AND ENTREPRENEURIAL ENGINE

2004
NEW DIRECTOR IS APPOINTED TO THE MUSEUM AT A TIME OF LOW VISITOR NUMBERS

2005
MEAL ACQUIRES ABBOTT'S HALL AND ADJACENT GARDENS

2006
FIRST GYPSY ARTS FESTIVAL IS HELD AND BONFIRE NIGHT ATTRACTS 3,000 PEOPLE

2007
MEAL SETS UP ABBOTT'S HALL ENTERPRISES AND STARTS NEW WORK –BASED LEARNING PROGRAMMES

2009
FIRST GOOD LIFE EVENT IS HELD; VISITORS ARE INVITED TO COMPOST, GROW-THEIR-OWN & COOK

2012
ABBOTT'S HALL PLANNED TO OPEN AS MULTI-USE CIVIC SPACE

SUPER-MARKET CARPARK

TOWN CENTRE

CURRENT ENTRANCE

PLANNED NEW ENTRANCE DIRECTLY INTO TOWN SQUARE

FISH POND

MUSEUM BUILDINGS & STORES

ABBOTT'S HALL

PLANNED PICNIC AND HANG-OUT AREAS WITH FREE WI-FI

PUBLIC ACCESS TO WETLAND MEADOWS WITH RIVERSIDE & WOODLAND WALKS

WORKSHOPS, PAINTING COURSES, TRAINING PROGRAMME & OTHER ACTIVITIES

ABBOTT'S HALL BARN: PICNIC EVENTS & FARMERS MARKET AREA

ABBOTT'S HALL FARM SHOP, FLOWER SHOP & VEGETABLE BOX SCHEME HQ

BISTRO AND CAFE WITH FREE ACCESS FOR TOWN RESIDENTS

COMMUNITY GARDENS WHERE VOLUNTEERS GROW PRODUCE FOR OWN CONSUMPTION OR SALE IN BARN SHOP

WALLED GARDENS RESTORED AND MAINTAINED BY VOLUNTEERS

THE STORY

Whereas many local history museums may struggle to be more than a 'cabinet of curiosities', an institutional reorganisation turned the Museum of East Anglian Life into a genuine 'civic museum' – a social enterprise and a new public space. Instead of struggling with low public funding and dwindling visitor numbers, the museum has established itself as a vibrant place in the town, as well as being a viable part of its economy and skills-training infrastructure.

The Museum of East Anglian Life (MEAL) was established as a traditional local history museum in 1967. On a 75-acre site at the edge of Stowmarket town centre, in Suffolk, it portrayed the area's social history through its re-erected historical buildings and an extensive collection of paintings and objects. However, in 2004, when Tony Butler arrived as director, visitor numbers were in decline. Inspired by the Coin Street Community Builders in London, Butler initiated a major transformation of the site and the museum's organisational structure. His ambition was 'to make the museum a place in which individuals are both beneficiaries and co-creators of their own space – where they can reflect on life and think about the world differently'.

A first move was simply to open up the museum grounds for community use by creating public picnic spaces and setting up a café in its premises. This was followed by a series of cultural initiatives, including musical and theatre events, a beer festival, a traditional music day and a Gypsy arts festival. Town residents became accustomed to seeing the museum as a place to hang out, be inspired and have a good time.

In 2007, MEAL set up Abbot's Hall Enterprises, a social enterprise that took over former New Deal for Communities programmes to provide training and therapeutic care services for young people, disabled adults, ex-offenders and long-term unemployed people. Most services provided are based on the museum's heritage work, and participants consequently contribute to its collections through the work they do, such as costume-making, horticulture, animal-keeping and building maintenance. Many of the products these programmes generate, such as baskets, flower arrangements and vegetables, are sold on in the Abbot's Hall Farm Shop. In 2010, MEAL won a public contract for Stowmarket floral display, not only bringing in income but also strengthening local pride.

MEAL has thus created a civic extension to the town centre's economy and public realm, re-defining what a museum can mean to a place and its people – building their capabilities and livelihoods, sustaining social networks, and providing a tangible form of localism.

IMPACT

Since 2006, MEAL has helped 40 individuals find jobs and 150 people have received accredited training. Building on this, in 2011 the museum will start a three-year Skills for the Future Scheme in partnership with other organisations, providing placements and courses in heritage skills. Additionally, each year, approximately 50,000 volunteer hours are provided, equivalent to nearly half a day per Stowmarket resident. More than 100 volunteers, many of them from disadvantaged backgrounds, take an active part in decision-making and project working groups. The museum has doubled its turnover and increased the number of visitors by 30%. Due to diversification in income streams, grant support from the local council has decreased from 50% of the budget to about a third.

KEY LESSONS

RECOGNISING THE PROTAGONISTS

Asset-holding civic entrepreneurs

Crucially, the new director realised that the biggest threat to the museum's survival was not low visitor numbers per se, but its under-utilisation as a community resource. Inspired by other social ventures, he worked with local people and service providers to integrate the museum into the social and physical fabric of the town – with a particular focus on vulnerable groups who have skills, ideas and needs but who do not profit fully from local cultural institutions.

RE-USING EXISTING ASSETS

Generating momentum through new uses

The physical changes required to open up the site to the community were relatively minor. Rather than embarking on an expensive building project, the museum generated momentum through increased activity, rethinking what could be done with the existing space to attract people. It provided facilities for everyday use and hosted locally rooted activities, including an independently run café, several picnic areas, a farm shop and cultural events. People can now engage with the museum without having to pay for entry. These changes have helped to embed the museum in the community whilst also linking it to local people's jobs and wider livelihoods. As more people are aware of the museum's existence, this has led to a substantial increase in visitor number.

AN OPEN ENDED APPROACH

Building a local action coalition

Through events and vocational training, the museum has strengthened its ties with the area. It has also engaged a wide range of people in its volunteering schemes and in co-producing content for the museum; more than 60% of volunteers are on work schemes or therapeutic care and resettlement programmes. Having built up a plethora of partnerships across the public, private and third sectors, MEAL is able to engage in a variety of activities without having to acquire specific skills in-house. This allows museum staff to continue focusing on cultural heritage whilst contributing significantly to the creation of new capabilities, jobs and experiences.

IN CONCLUSION

How do we shift the role of local cultural organisations towards an ever more active social and economic role in our places? The Museum of East Anglian Life shows how, by opening up their physical assets and organisational infrastructure, they can use the core strength of their cultural offer as a welcoming platform for participation. This creates not just a richer public realm but also builds skills, jobs and a shared sense of belonging.

OTHER EXAMPLES

Horniman Museum, London, UK, 2002

…is an anthropology and natural history museum that trains and employs local people in museum collection management, which allows the museum to reach out and collaborate with otherwise hard-to-reach communities.

Green Estate, Sheffield, UK, 2004

…started out as an environment and heritage project in a deprived inner-city neighbourhood, and evolved into a social enterprise providing business and employment opportunities in green-space maintenance.

Le Jardin Aux Habitants, Paris, France, 2002

…is an allotment strip to the side of the Palais de Tokyo contemporary art museum; maintained by a gardening association and open to the public, it changes the dynamic between the museum and the street.

Timber wall panels in the Makar workshop. The sheep's wool shown to the right is used to insulate the panels before going on site

16

NEIL SUTHERLAND ARCHITECTS

AN INTEGRATED TIMBER BUILDING PRACTICE
INVERNESS, UNITED KINGDOM

'In Scotland we have had to re-learn the value and possibilities of the resources we have here in our landscape. Neil Sutherland Architects stand out amongst a great range of people and practices now working together to broaden the skills and evidence base of what we can produce in Scotland.'

Peter Wilson, The Wood Studio, Forest Products Research Institute, Edinburgh Napier University

PRIMARY
CONSTRUCTION
MATERIALS
SOURCED FROM

50 MILE RADIUS

AVERAGE
APPRENTICESHIPS

2 X
LENGTH OF
UK STANDARD

81.5%
AVERAGE
TRANSPORT
EMISSIONS
SAVINGS THROUGH
LOCAL SOURCING

BUILDING A GROUNDED APPROACH TO WORK, INNOVATION AND SUSTAINABILITY

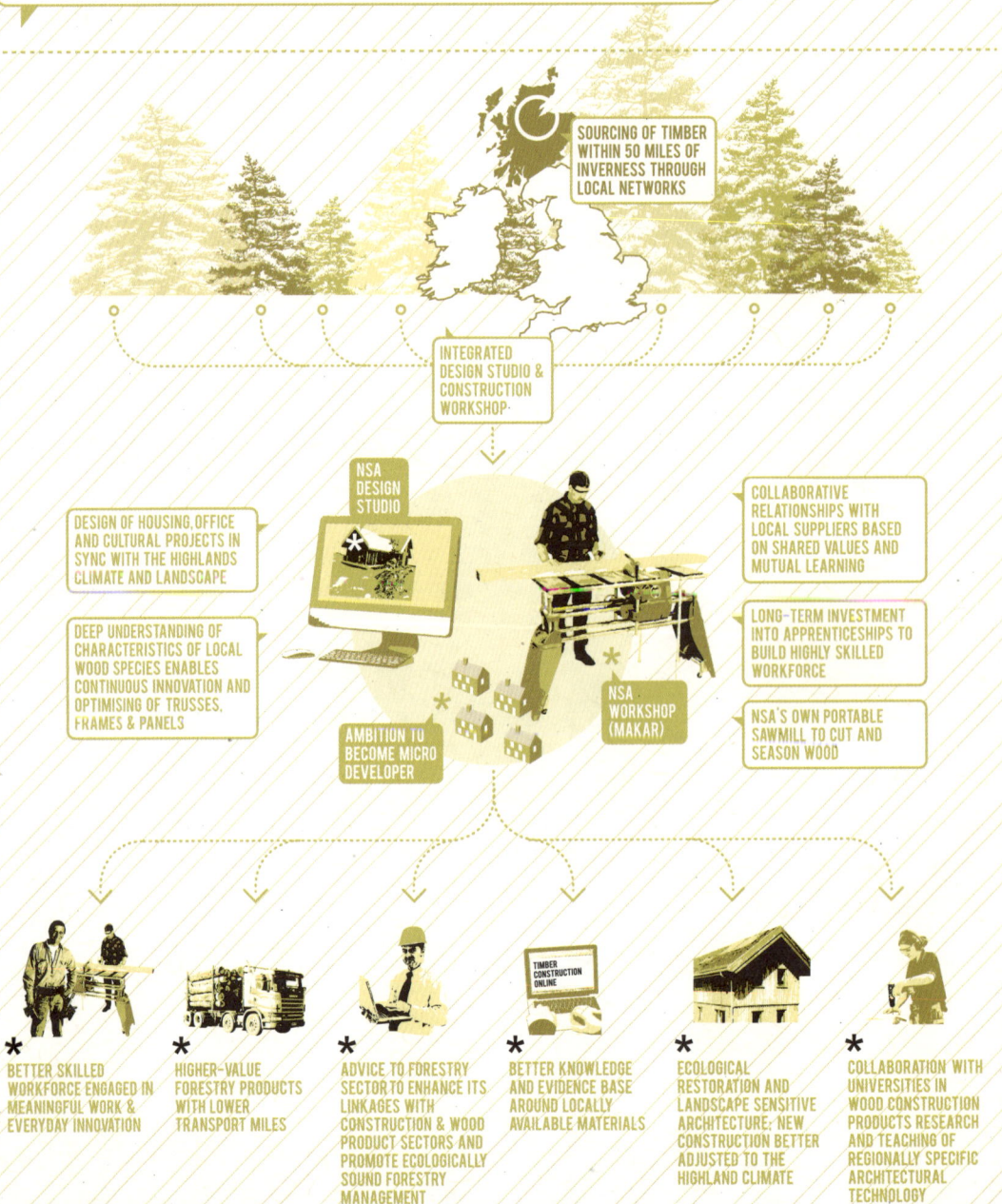

SOURCING OF TIMBER WITHIN 50 MILES OF INVERNESS THROUGH LOCAL NETWORKS

INTEGRATED DESIGN STUDIO & CONSTRUCTION WORKSHOP

NSA DESIGN STUDIO

DESIGN OF HOUSING, OFFICE AND CULTURAL PROJECTS IN SYNC WITH THE HIGHLANDS CLIMATE AND LANDSCAPE

DEEP UNDERSTANDING OF CHARACTERISTICS OF LOCAL WOOD SPECIES ENABLES CONTINUOUS INNOVATION AND OPTIMISING OF TRUSSES, FRAMES & PANELS

AMBITION TO BECOME MICRO DEVELOPER

NSA WORKSHOP (MAKAR)

COLLABORATIVE RELATIONSHIPS WITH LOCAL SUPPLIERS BASED ON SHARED VALUES AND MUTUAL LEARNING

LONG-TERM INVESTMENT INTO APPRENTICESHIPS TO BUILD HIGHLY SKILLED WORKFORCE

NSA'S OWN PORTABLE SAWMILL TO CUT AND SEASON WOOD

* BETTER SKILLED WORKFORCE ENGAGED IN MEANINGFUL WORK & EVERYDAY INNOVATION

* HIGHER-VALUE FORESTRY PRODUCTS WITH LOWER TRANSPORT MILES

* ADVICE TO FORESTRY SECTOR TO ENHANCE ITS LINKAGES WITH CONSTRUCTION & WOOD PRODUCT SECTORS AND PROMOTE ECOLOGICALLY SOUND FORESTRY MANAGEMENT

* BETTER KNOWLEDGE AND EVIDENCE BASE AROUND LOCALLY AVAILABLE MATERIALS

TIMBER CONSTRUCTION ONLINE

* ECOLOGICAL RESTORATION AND LANDSCAPE SENSITIVE ARCHITECTURE; NEW CONSTRUCTION BETTER ADJUSTED TO THE HIGHLAND CLIMATE

* COLLABORATION WITH UNIVERSITIES IN WOOD CONSTRUCTION PRODUCTS RESEARCH AND TEACHING OF REGIONALLY SPECIFIC ARCHITECTURAL TECHNOLOGY

THE STORY

When Neil Sutherland started an architecture practice in the Scottish Highlands, he realised that the local construction industry was unable to support his triple ambition of building with locally sourced, non-toxic, ecologically high-performance wood. He decided to take matters into his own hands. Twenty years on, Neil Sutherland Architects (NSA) is a unique, vertically integrated architecture, construction and research practice, and Sutherland himself part of a growing innovation network in the Scottish wood sector, deeply rooted in the Highland landscape whilst engaging with the challenges of contemporary house building.

Innovation is not the word he prefers to use – instead, he speaks about familiarisation, emphasising that creativity and product improvement happens in the everyday refinement of products through a meaningful and integrated work process. The journey to his practice is exemplary for this. Having quit school early and worked in engineering apprenticeships before embarking on architecture, Sutherland spent an exchange period at the Illinois Institute of Technology – learning directly from the heirs of the famous Bauhaus tradition of integrated but forward-looking craftsmanship. Back in Scotland, he first worked on an environmental restoration project in the western Highlands before setting up his practice in Inverness. His approach to architecture and building, therefore, is decidedly hands-on.

Acquiring a mobile sawmill and setting up an integrated construction company – Makar – within the practice

made sense from this point of view. With a collaborative team that includes experienced joiners, NSA / Makar can carry out practical research into making structural beam and panel systems that are beautifully detailed, more energy efficient and quick to build. Integral to this is investment in the workforce – initially Sutherland employed German carpenters-in-training, as the local workforce lacked the necessary skills, but now the practice has a very productive relationship with the Scottish government's apprenticeship scheme. On average, apprentices – a remarkable proportion of whom are in their late 20s or early 30s, rather than school-leavers – stay for four years. This is much longer than required by the government scheme but necessary to acquire a broad range of skills across the production chain. Many of them end up with jobs at Makar.

Diverse collaborative networks have always been central to the practice – local social networks and word of mouth, for example, are crucial to obtaining good-quality Douglas fir from the region to reduce transport cost; most of his primary materials come from within 50 miles from Inverness. Increasingly, Sutherland is also linking into wider networks of research, innovation and reform. He works with the Wood Studio at Edinburgh Napier University on the development of innovative timber products, processes and systems, integrating best practice from around the world to support a more purposeful, competitive and dynamic industry. Sutherland is also an adviser to the regional Forest Forum – with the aim of getting people in the forestry, construction, and product development to work and learn more closely together. He is also scaling up practice-led research workshops, with EU funding, to develop a next generation of frame and panel systems to increase his capacity for off-site construction, standards and performance testing, and cost reduction. In the next few years, he wants to move from being able to build five homes a year to about 20.

Sutherland's research and consultancy work is also leading him into planning reform and landscape architecture, as part of an ambition to build pathways for place-making that are truly in sync with the local landscape, climate and ecology, and that reduce impact on utilities and infrastructure.

IMPACT

NSA has built a diverse output of private homes as well as office projects, shops, a fishing lodge and an education centre. Between them, the design studio and the integrated construction practice now employ about 20 people. According to Peter Wilson of the Wood Studio at Edinburgh Napier University, NSA has contributed to a much better understanding of local forestry products since the early 2000s. Whilst the volume housebuilding sector has not yet adopted a wholesale shift in approach, more and more small developers and contractors are shifting their orientation towards innovative, high-value local materials and products.

KEY LESSONS

RECOGNISING THE PROTAGONISTS

RE-USING EXISTING ASSETS

GENERATING CHANGE THROUGH NETWORKS

Investing in local value

The key to the development of NSA has been an effort to create the local relationships needed to work productively in the area. Apart from convincing local planners that his approach was not only viable but valuable, Sutherland has invested time in looking for local collaborators. By being explicit about his quality ambition, work ethos and values, he created a network of local businesses that are not just suppliers but also engage in mutual learning and product development – such as for better large triple-glazed windows. Similarly, his deep investment in long-term apprenticeships is essentially a way to grow his own workforce and create fertile ground for the practice to flourish.

Recognising latent opportunities

NSA's approach is rooted in a realisation that local building materials were unnecessarily overlooked by the volume housebuilding industry in Scotland. In the post-war period, timber-framed homes were increasingly produced using imported wood, leading to ingrained perceptions that local timber was not suitable for use in the construction industry. Moreover, a segmented approach to research into design, construction and materials had led to a de-skilling of the workforce and a lack of innovation in both the construction and forestry sectors. NSA's research and practice is part of a broader shift to broadening the skills and evidence base to reverse this trend and rebuild awareness both in the industry itself and across the education and research sector.

A re-emerging innovation field

Whereas Sutherland's practice is deeply rooted in the realities of the local landscape, he is part of an expanding group of design practices, research institutions and sector innovation networks that together are building a new awareness of the role of local raw materials in the area's innovation economy. Other Scottish architects, such as Dualchas and Rural Studio, both on the Isle of Skye, are also working with Edinburgh's Wood Studio on projects taking the local landscape, climate and available resources as a starting point. The Wood Studio itself is part of the Forest Products Research Institute, which works with the Scottish Forestry Commission, Scottish Enterprise and other universities to diversify and innovate in the sector. Together these organisations are transforming perceptions of the Scottish wood sector, demonstrating its potential as an innovative, high-value industry.

IN CONCLUSION

How do we maintain and strengthen a broader shared understanding of what it takes to be creative on the everyday workfloor, right across the different sections of our economy? The example of Neil Sutherland Architects shows that those firms who put meaningful work and workforce investment first can build an enterprise economy that is sustainable and innovative in the full sense of both words – and how local and regional collaborations are integral to achieving this.

OTHER EXAMPLES

The ABLE (Andrew Barker Lepton Employment) Project, Wakefield, UK, 2002
...was initiated by the Green Business Network; this 'Cardboard to Caviar' project is an inland fish farm centred around a closed-loop waste and material cycle, which also is an education and social employment centre.

Delabole Slate Company Ltd, Cornwall, UK, 1999
...is a quarrying and manufacturing company that makes bespoke products for the building and home improvement trade from the oldest slate mine in England; its product and process innovation focus on waste minimisation.

Gripple, Sheffield, UK, 1986
...is an employee-owned company making specialist wire and tensioner products for agricultural and industrial use; its values-driven approach and business success has led two of its supplier companies to adopt employee-ownership arrangements.

Cattle grazing along the M1 near Nottingham

17

NOTTINGHAM UNIVERSITY HOSPITALS

SUSTAINABLE FOOD PROCUREMENT
NOTTINGHAM, UNITED KINGDOM

'We worked especially hard to convince local food suppliers that the hospital is not some kind of mythical organisation'

John Hughes, Catering Manager, Nottingham University Hospitals NHS Trust

95% LOCALLY SOURCED MEAT

100% LOCALLY SOURCED MILK

150,000 SAVED FOOD MILES / YEAR

£0 ADDITIONAL COST TO NHS

CHANGING PUBLIC SECTOR PROCUREMENT TO ACHIEVE BETTER OUTCOMES

* STANDARD NHS FOOD OFFER

* EXCESSIVE FOOD MILES DUE TO GLOBAL SUPPLY CHAIN

* DECLINING LOCAL BUSINESSES & FARMS

* STANDARD NHS WORKING PROCEDURE

ISSUES

+

defra
Department for Environment Food and Rural Affairs

* USING EXISTING LEGISLATION

* FACE-TO-FACE VISITS TO FARMERS

WELCOME !

* 'OPEN HOUSE' EVENTS – INVITING FARMERS INTO THE HOSPITAL

NHU SUSTAINABLE PROCUREMENT
Local Farms A1
Low CO2 Only
Local Suppliers

* LOCAL PRODUCE PREFERENCED BY INCLUDING ENVIRONMENTAL COST IN TENDER CRITERIA

TACTICS

=

* MORE NUTRITIOUS FOOD

OUR FARM SHOP is now open.

* REJUVENATION OF LOCAL FARM ECONOMY

JAN

* SEASONAL MENUS HAVE INSPIRED STAFF

CO_2

* SIGNIFICANT CARBON SAVINGS

OUTCOMES

THE STORY

It isn't just the legislation that matters – it's the way that committed individuals make it work and bring it to life by their personal engagement. Adopting protocols set out in 2003 in the UK government's Public Sector Food Procurement Initiative, the catering team at the city campus of Nottingham University Hospitals NHS Trust (NUH) decided to see whether they could reduce food miles by increasingly sourcing food locally.

Catering manager John Hughes initiated the changes by modifying contract specifications in accordance with the recommendations from the Department for Environment, Food and Rural Affairs (Defra) and using them to their full potential. This meant including environmental requirements in the tenders instead of purely asking for the cheapest product.

Crucially, the catering team went beyond Defra's minimum requirements by engaging with local food-producers on a face-to-face basis. After all, reducing bureaucratic hurdles alone does not change the much-held perception that hospitals are impossible to penetrate for small businesses. Apart from an 'open day', where suppliers could meet the team and get a better understanding of the trust's food needs, the catering team also went out to local farms and spoke with farmers in the area. This helped disperse the myth that the NHS accreditation was unattainable for small food producers. By helping local suppliers to receive such accreditation, the team became civic entrepreneurs in their own right.

Personal commitment and passion set the culture for a different approach. This was further enabled by the NUH trust's Good Corporate Citizen Initiative, which had confirmed the importance of sustainability principles in 2002 without prescribing how they should be delivered in its hospitals. Thus, the initiative won the essential backing of the trust's board.

IMPACT

As a consequence of the Sustainable Food Procurement Initiative, the hospital is now fully supplied with milk from a farm in the region, and 95% of its meat is sourced through a local abattoir that aggregates the supply streams from small meat suppliers in the East Midlands. On standardised calculations, this has helped the hospital save 150,000 food miles per year; the quality of the produce has greatly improved, even as costs have stayed the same. At the same time, the initiative has helped sustain local agricultural production and saved at least one pig farm from closing.

KEY LESSONS

RECOGNISING THE PROTAGONISTS

Embedded civic entrepreneurs

The NUH catering team, working within Defra guidelines, invested in engagement with local farmers, going the extra mile to reduce barriers. According to John Hughes, face-to-face contact between food producers and the hospital led farmers to realise 'that the hospital is not some kind of mythical organisation and that our requirements are no higher than supermarkets'. The project follows existing regulation so the catering team are reluctant to make claims to radicalism – but it has built the networks for a civic economy through a pioneering outreach approach. Although the same Defra guidelines have not led to change in other trusts, the NUH initiative proves what can be achieved.

PARTICIPATION BEYOND CONSULTATION

Shared culture change

Internally, the NUH initiative necessitated a culture change within the catering team, who had to become increasingly flexible and use their professional creativity to accommodate seasonality, and together create new practices. Such changes were, however, communicated as a positive challenge by the catering manager, rather than a dreary obstacle. The restructuring of the process did not have any negative financial consequences for the NUH and no extra funding or infrastructure was required.

RECOGNISING WHERE VALUE LIES

Changing the metrics

Including environmental metrics (lowering food miles and carbon footprint) in tender requirements was an important condition for the success of the project; this created a level playing field between big established providers and smaller local business. This deliberate steering on public value outcomes was based on a shared recognition of a different way of creating value, which helped to enable a relatively smooth organisational shift.

IN CONCLUSION

If we agree that more sustainable supply chains are integral to a truly civic economy, how can large public organisations play their part? The NUH Sustainable Food Procurement Initiative shows where 'scale efficiencies' need to give way to devolving leadership within larger systems. This is essential to unleash the capacity of individuals and small teams to make a difference – breathing life into existing regulation for the benefit of the local economy and its use of resources.

OTHER EXAMPLES

Raploch Urban Regeneration Company, Stirling, UK, 2004
...is an estate regeneration project that has achieved a high degree of community benefits through smart contract specification within EU legal requirements, requiring contractors to employ a large ratio of young jobseekers and long-term unemployed adults, most of whom will be local residents.

Whole Life Costing & CO₂ Tool, Fife, UK, 2009
...is a public procurement toolkit developed by Fife Council and Forum for the Future to understand the total cost and impact of a product over the entire contract period from its purchase through to its disposal.

O2 Eco Rating, UK, 2010
...is a mobile phone sustainability rating system developed by the communications company O2 for internal use but which customers can now use to make more informed decisions about the environmental credentials of phones.

The Jodok restaurant, run by the Olinda Co-operative and the main point of entrance to the grounds of the former psychiatric hospital

18

OLINDA PSYCHIATRIC HOSPITAL

A CLOSED INSTITUTION OPENED UP
MILAN, ITALY

'Olinda has created unprecedented links between care and support for the weaker segments of the population and the cultural opportunities for the social enjoyment of the city as a whole.'

Tommaso Vitale, Associate Professor, Sciences Po Paris

35,000
VISITORS FOR OLINDA'S FIRST SUMMER FESTIVAL

90%
INCOME FROM PRODUCTION ACTIVITIES IN FABBRICA DI OLINDA

220
VOLUNTEERS ALONGSIDE 29 STAFF MEMBERS ACROSS 2 SOCIAL ENTERPRISES

TRANSFORMING A HOSPITAL INTO A NEIGHBOURHOOD RESOURCE

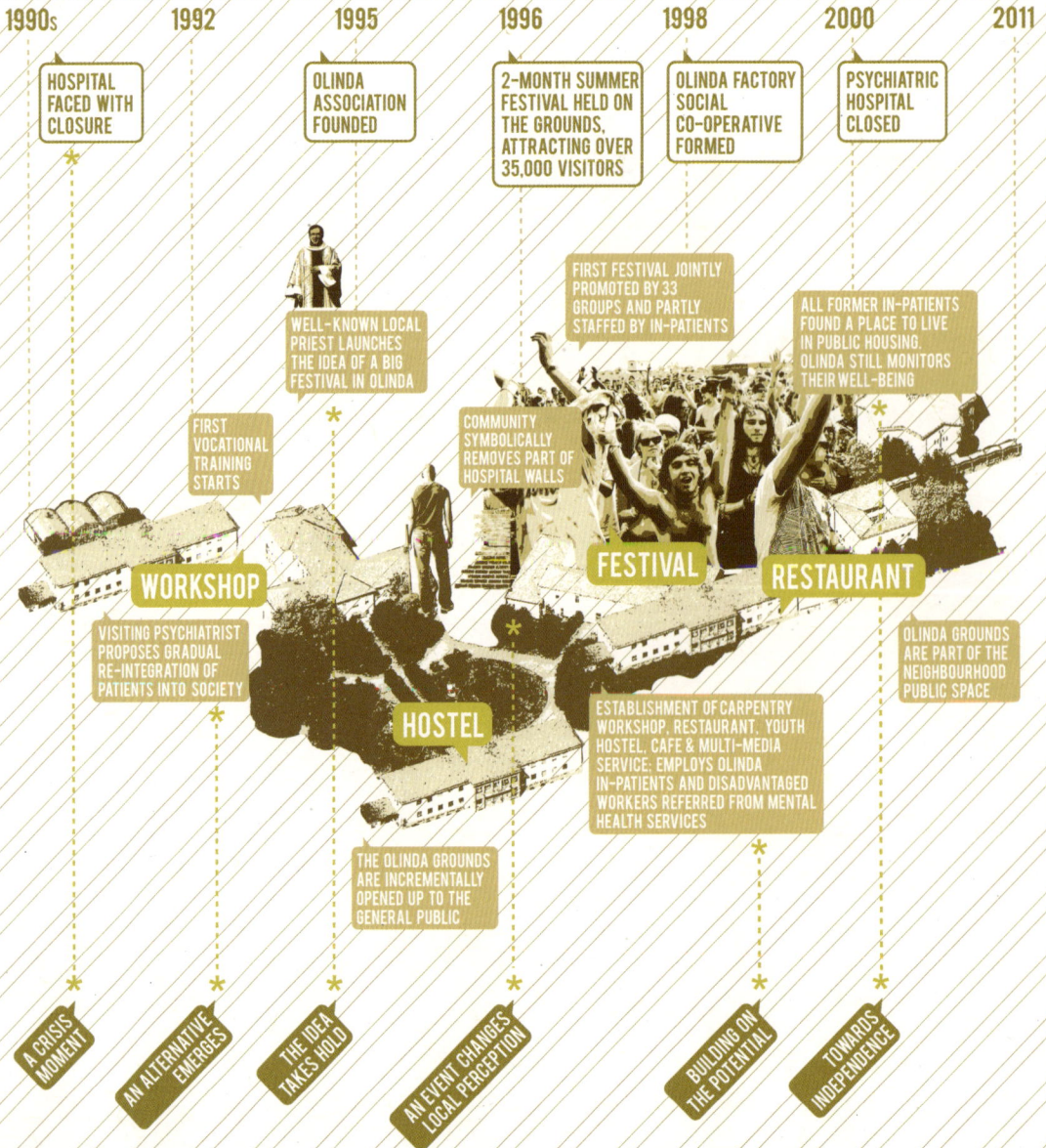

1990s — **1992** — **1995** — **1996** — **1998** — **2000** — **2011**

HOSPITAL FACED WITH CLOSURE

OLINDA ASSOCIATION FOUNDED

2-MONTH SUMMER FESTIVAL HELD ON THE GROUNDS, ATTRACTING OVER 35,000 VISITORS

OLINDA FACTORY SOCIAL CO-OPERATIVE FORMED

PSYCHIATRIC HOSPITAL CLOSED

WELL-KNOWN LOCAL PRIEST LAUNCHES THE IDEA OF A BIG FESTIVAL IN OLINDA

FIRST FESTIVAL JOINTLY PROMOTED BY 33 GROUPS AND PARTLY STAFFED BY IN-PATIENTS

ALL FORMER IN-PATIENTS FOUND A PLACE TO LIVE IN PUBLIC HOUSING. OLINDA STILL MONITORS THEIR WELL-BEING

FIRST VOCATIONAL TRAINING STARTS

COMMUNITY SYMBOLICALLY REMOVES PART OF HOSPITAL WALLS

WORKSHOP

FESTIVAL

RESTAURANT

VISITING PSYCHIATRIST PROPOSES GRADUAL RE-INTEGRATION OF PATIENTS INTO SOCIETY

OLINDA GROUNDS ARE PART OF THE NEIGHBOURHOOD PUBLIC SPACE

HOSTEL

ESTABLISHMENT OF CARPENTRY WORKSHOP, RESTAURANT, YOUTH HOSTEL, CAFE & MULTI-MEDIA SERVICE: EMPLOYS OLINDA IN-PATIENTS AND DISADVANTAGED WORKERS REFERRED FROM MENTAL HEALTH SERVICES

THE OLINDA GROUNDS ARE INCREMENTALLY OPENED UP TO THE GENERAL PUBLIC

A CRISIS MOMENT

AN ALTERNATIVE EMERGES

THE IDEA TAKES HOLD

AN EVENT CHANGES LOCAL PERCEPTION

BUILDING ON THE POTENTIAL

TOWARDS INDEPENDENCE

THE STORY

The relation between large institutions and their neighbourhoods is often ambiguous, as the presence of the former may not always benefit the latter. However, when institutional reform prompted change at the Olinda Psychiatric Hospital in Milan, the surrounding low-income suburb also profited. A previously stigmatised, closed institution was transformed into a new public space for former patients as well as for the wider metropolitan area.

In 1992, with the hospital scheduled for closure within the decade, a visiting psychiatrist proposed the gradual reintroduction of patients into society at large, and eventually the health professionals set up the Associazone Olinda to provide vocational training for patients. Battling local authority scepticism, a core group of entrepreneurial innovators – creative professionals, artists, health professionals, technicians, academics, market entrepreneurs and social workers – gradually opened up the closed site and turned it into a multi-purpose space. Its physical environment was made more welcoming and integrated into the neighbourhood.

A crucial step was Olinda's first summer festival in the hospital grounds, in 1996. Organised in collaboration with patients, the festival lasted over two months, attracted more than 35,000 visitors from across the region, and included the symbolic tearing down of a piece of the wall around the psychiatric wards. The success of the event worked to break down significant barriers (both physical and perceptual) between the hospital and a local community that had initially been wary of the project. The festival also helped to engage the wider public in the hospital's problems and engender public debates about its future, thereby becoming a mobilising event for action.

In 1998, the association created the Fabbrica di Olinda, a social co-operative staffed by patients and other local people normally excluded from the labour market. The co-operative included a carpentry workshop, a restaurant, a youth hostel, a café and a multimedia service. These activities ensured a continued stream of revenue, even as the hospital's core funding stopped. The hospital closed as planned in 2000, but the Olinda association and the co-operative continue to ensure that former in-patients are safely and appropriately housed, while also providing them with opportunities for wider social engagement. The grounds remain a vibrant public place in the neighbourhood despite pressures from real estate development interests, and an on-going struggle to raise funds for necessary capital investment.

IMPACT

Today, the former hospital site continues to host the Olinda association and the co-operative, which have increasingly diversified into the cultural sector while still employing former patients. The grounds are also used as public space for the local community. In the years after its official closure as a hospital, Olinda has grown to employ 29 staff members and also works with 50 permanent and 170 occasional volunteers. Since 2000, most of the turnover (90% in the co-op) revolves around Olinda's production activities. This has effectively reduced Olinda's dependency on volatile public funding and increased its financial resilience, allowing it to continue as a third sector organisation.

KEY LESSONS

PARTICIPATION BEYOND CONSULTATION

Engaging patients and the wider public

The Olinda case shows the benefits of engaging in economic activities within mental health institutions. Instead of being perceived as passive victims, in-patients were seen as resourceful individuals. This enabled them to contribute constructively while also improving their own well-being and ultimately supporting them to re-enter society at large. As a co-produced civic in-stitution, Olinda became a convivial public space and festival site open local residents, irrespective of their backgrounds, which transformed perceptions of the hospital in the community. Residents started to use Olinda's open spaces for community activities and used the co-op's services to improve their livelihoods.

GENERATING CHANGE THROUGH NETWORKS

The role of external innovators

Many changes at Olinda were initiated by a psychiatrist from Rome, who belonged to the 'de-institutionalisation movement'. He brought with him not only valuable ideas and strategies but also vital relationships, acquired from his previous experience in transforming psychiatric institutions and starting up social entrepreneurships within the sector. As a networked outsider, he was able to deal with the institution in a new way and to build a broader action coalition that broke through the conservatism of Milan's mental health policy. He was also able to draw on funding and support organisations outside the city, including regional and EU-wide programmes.

AN OPEN ENDED APPROACH

Entrepreneurial diversification

Rather than following a detailed strategic plan, Olinda evolved a variety of social and economic activities in response to local needs and opportunities. This entrepreneurial diversification has ensured a relatively steady stream of income, even as individual sources continue to be contingent. Decision-making structures aim to be open and democratic, for example by involving both employees and volunteers. This creates scope for critical self-evaluation, learning and evolutionary development of activities.

IN CONCLUSION

How do we reconfigure large-scale public institutions so that they genuinely improve the neighbourhoods that host them? The story of Olinda shows that a crisis moment – such as the threat of closure – can be a catalyst for joining up the purpose of an organisation with that of the wider locality. Such collaborations only happen if we maintain the openness of mind and organisational porosity to embrace the type of unlikely combinations that create gains for all.

OTHER EXAMPLES

Solihull Mind, Knowle, UK, 1995
...undertook an 'ecotherapy' project that has transformed a derelict fly-tipping site into an organic garden, football field and boules court, with the help of local people experiencing mental distress.

Arc (Arts for Recovery in the Community), Stockport, UK, 1998
...is a community centre and social enterprise that incorporates art and design studios and a gallery to help people with mental health problems to be socially integrated in the community.

Favela Adventures, Rio de Janeiro, Brazil, 2008
...is a community-operated tourism enterprise that has reduced the stigma associated with the slum area of Rocinha by inviting city dwellers and tourists to events and interactive tours run by local people.

Night-time scene from One Love City during the Outgames 2009

19

ONE LOVE CITY

A CROWD-SOURCED PUBLIC EVENT
COPENHAGEN, DENMARK

'I wish it had stayed, because it was so refreshing with an open space smack in the middle of the city, where you could just hang out by the water and listen to music. I didn't climb around or actively use the space, like other people did, I just liked hanging around it. For some reason, good people seemed to flock there.'

Nola Grace Gaardmand, Copenhagener

20,000
VISITORS IN TEN DAYS

50%
OF INSTALLATION MADE FROM RECYCLED MATERIALS

36
COMMUNITY & CULTURAL ORGANISATIONS CURATED ONE LOVE CITY TOGETHER

BRINGING PUBLIC SPACE TO LIFE THROUGH OPEN CURATION

SUMMER 2008

SUMMER 2009

ROYAL DANISH LIBRARY OFFERS ITS SQUARE FOR USAGE DURING THE OUTGAMES LGBT EVENT

AARHUS ACCEPTS INVITATION BY OUTGAMES TO CREATE EVENT ON KIERKE-GAARD SQUARE

KULTURHUS AARHUS TAKES ON THE PROJECT & ASKS LOCAL FILM-MAKER TO CURATE IT

CURATOR GATHERS ECLECTIC COALITION OF ARTISTS, BUSINESSES AND COMMUNITY GROUPS TO CO-CREATE ONE LOVE CITY

ONE LOVE CITY SPACE AND EVENT PROGRAMME CONSTRUCTED THROUGH CROWD-SOURCING AND KEPT FLEXIBLE TO ENCOURAGE SPONTANEOUS CONTRIBUTIONS

* ONE LOVE CITY

INSTALLATIONS BY 20 ARTISTS

* ROYAL DANISH LIBRARY

RECYCLED SHIPPING CONTAINER USED AS GALLERY BY DAY AND MAKESHIFT HOTEL BY NIGHT

TEMPORARY PUBLIC DIVING BOARD

MINIATURE PLAYGROUND FOR KIDS

* FOOD TASTING EVENT BY AARHUS MASTER CHEFS

* FOOD & DRINK BY AARHUSIAN CAFES AND BARS

* WOOD SALVAGED FROM DISCARDED SCHOOL GYM FLOORBOARDS IN AARHUS

* 'PROUD' SECOND-HAND BOOKS AND 'FUND' LOCAL ARTISAN PRODUCED DESIGN ITEMS

* KONG GULEROD ORGANIC & LOCALLY SOURCED FRUIT & VEG MARKET

* STAGE WITH GIGS PROGRAMMED BY LOCAL SHOPS, AND 'OPEN SLOTS' FOR IMPROMPTU EVENTS

* 40 PROFESSIONALS, STUDENTS AND FRIENDS PERFORM THE WORLD'S BIGGEST SYNCHRONISED SWIM

THE STORY

Grand but empty public squares and free but intimidating art galleries are an issue in many contemporary cities. But for 10 days in the summer of 2009, one of Copenhagen's biggest new squares was transformed into a lively cultural marketplace, a platform for participation and a social meeting space. One Love City was the result of a collaborative effort between the public sector, private businesses and a broad coalition of community organisations.

The miniature city was assembled on Søren Kierkegaard Square, a large open space in front of the new and imposing Royal Danish Library. Curated in connection with the World Outgames, an international lesbian, gay, bisexual and transgender (LGBT) event held in Copenhagen in 2009, One Love City was co-funded and co-produced by local art, design and architecture communities, as well as members of the city's LGBT community, local businesses, the Kulturhus Aarhus and the Royal Danish Library. This coalition provided the cultural stewardship to transform the new square into a sociable space where an open-ended cultural programme could be tested and experimented with, and that could bridge across the diverse social groups in the city.

Cities across the world had been invited to inhabit Copenhagen's squares for the duration of the Outgames, an invitation the mayor of Aarhus personally accepted on behalf of his city. The independent, council-funded organisation Kulturhus Aarhus agreed to take on the fundraising and curating role, and from the very beginning it was agreed that local businesses had to be included in the collaboration alongside representatives of the LGBT community, artists and architects. This broad coalition was coordinated by film-maker Morten Lundgaard, who

advocated an eclectic and open-ended approach as a way of curating 'life, rather than just another boring queer art exhibition'. As a result, the cultural programme was deliberately open to the impromptu contributions of artists, visitors and locals; the space became an evolving playground and a civic platform inviting people continuously to co-produce new experiences.

One Love City became the central meeting place for Copenhageners during the Outgames; shops, bars and lounge areas helped to draw people in from the streets, thereby reducing the division between the Outgames' mainly LGBT participants, the art communities and the general public.

The event was only intended to exist for 10 days, so its creators wanted it to have as small an environmental footprint as possible. Inspired by the Burning Man festival's 'Leave No Trace' principle, the designers created an adventure playground-inspired installation made from at least 50% recycled materials including pallets, containers, scaffolding and wooden boards from old school gym floors.

IMPACT

Beyond generating healthy revenue for the local businesses involved, One Love City was successful because it facilitated shared learning: for many of the cultural and public institutions involved it proved a catalyst for rethinking their own cultural and public space strategies. The Royal Danish Library subsequently developed innovative engagement programmes to diversify the use of the library and change how it invites people in; its first annual 'Back to School' party for university students attracted more than 2,000 students. The project also led organisations in Aarhus to connect and engage in long-term partnerships and projects. This has included the on-going urban transformation of the four-hectare Freight Yard Area into a cultural quarter. According to Pia Buchardt, director of Kulturhus Aarhus, 'One Love City was a networking building project that created a platform for future collaborations around urban development in Aarhus, and allowed us to rethink and expand our notion of urbanism'.

KEY LESSONS

RECOGNISING THE PROTAGONISTS

Networked civic entrepreneurs

A large civic coalition adopted and promoted the project, under the brokering role of a respected cultural organisation. However, instead of seeing it as an in-house 'project management' task, the Kulturhus Aarhus hired a highly networked curator to bring together and steer the diverse contributors. By involving many different groups in the co-production of One Love City, the coordinator was able to let them generate a diversity of activities loosely held together under an umbrella theme but open to initiatives from people outside the primary programme.

AN OPEN ENDED APPROACH

Bringing public space to life

Whilst Søren Kirkegaard Square was the outcome of a high-profile public redevelopment project, it was recognised that a plan-led approach would not be sufficient to make it a success. Hence Kulturhus Aarhus decided to focus primarily on creating an open-ended social platform where different approaches to activating the public realm could be tested. Attracting footfall was crucial – people could then, when it suited them, engage with and participate in the cultural offer. One Love City therefore featured shops, casual hang-out spaces, nooks, playgrounds and bars, in addition to galleries and a performance stage. This worked to reduce barriers to participation, as the city reduced the sense of intimidation often associated with arts spaces.

THE EXPERIENCE OF PLACE

Celebrating makeshift culture

One Love City articulated the environmental and social aspirations behind the project – as well as its organising logic – through the 'open platform' physical structure of the installation. This was enabled by the Royal Danish Library, which had given the organisers substantial and unprecedented freedoms to experiment with the space on a temporary basis. The design created a 'junk playground' where the public were invited to participate and explore – a contrast with the high-spec design of the Square itself. The quirky use of recycled materials helped convey a playful makeshift ethos – including, for instance, gallery spaces that were converted into clubs in the evening and impromptu hotels by night.

IN CONCLUSION

How to fulfil the promise of public space as a platform for shared experiences that bridge across social divides? One Love City shows one way of doing this: by configuring events not as spectacle but as collaborative platforms connecting a wide range of contributors and participants. Such events allow us to experiment and test ways to answer an important challenge: animating the spaces we already have instead of always relying on new capital investment.

OTHER EXAMPLES

Urban Beach, Bristol, UK, 2007
...was a public-private collaborative project where an underused car park between the city centre and a low-income neighbourhood was transformed into a public beach for six weeks.

The Image Mill, Quebec City, Canada, 2008
...is a periodic event supported by Quebec City Council, where films and images from the city's history are projected onto the 600m x 30m façade of a large grain silo in the harbour.

Wick Curiosity Shop, London, UK, 2008
...is an ever-expanding collection of local produce, memorabilia, oral history, songs and stories from or about Hackney Wick in East London, initiated by the artist collective Public Works with Hilary Powell. It includes an online record and an evolving range of events.

Jon Coffe doing a shift as a cashier at The People's Supermarket

20

THE PEOPLE'S SUPERMARKET

A SOCIAL VENTURE SUPERMARKET
LONDON, UNITED KINGDOM

'It's a very diverse neighbourhood, and I guess everyone shops differently. But with The People's Supermarket we don't just have a shop; we have a place where we can come together as a community to talk about food and deal more responsibly with its supply. I've met young people here who didn't know how to peel a potato but now they can come and learn to cook in The People's Kitchen.'

Suki Jobson, The People's Supermarket member and kitchen volunteer

1,000
MEMBERS
AFTER ONE YEAR

60%
OF MEMBERSHIP
FROM LOCAL AREA

10%
DISCOUNT ON
GROCERIES FOR
MEMBERS

CREATING A HYBRID VALUE LOCAL SHOP

2009   **2010**   **2011**

INITIATED   OPENED   GROWING

* MEMBER VOLUNTEER TIME
* MEMBER CO-GOVERNANCE
* CHARITY SUPPORT (APPRENTICESHIP PROGRAMMES)
* DONATED MATERIALS
* SKILLS & TIME DONATION
* SMALL-SCALE PUBLIC SUBSIDY
* INTEREST-FREE LOANS

MIXED-MODE INPUTS

The People's Supermarket

WE NOW HAVE 500+ MEMBERS

SOCIAL RETURN

* SUSTAINABLE & LOCALLY SOURCED FOOD
* AFFORDABLE & HIGH-QUALITY GROCERIES
* LOCAL SAY OVER RE-INVESTING OF PROFITS
* BUILDING SKILLS
* MINIMISING FOOD WASTE
* BUILDING LOCAL SOCIAL CAPITAL VIA VOLUNTEERING AND EVENTS
* PLATFORM FOR OTHER VENTURES

THE STORY

In a central London neighbourhood with a diverse population of both low-income groups and high earners, a recession-hit budget chain grocers was replaced by The People's Supermarket, a grocery owned and managed by members but open to all, and committed to selling good-quality, locally sourced products at an affordable price. In return for a small fee (£25 a year) and four hours of volunteering a month, members get a 10% discount.

The People's Supermarket was the initiative of a group of social entrepreneurs with a track record in community-driven regeneration, sustainability, food-related innovation and grocery retailing. Aiming to reduce food poverty and health inequality by providing affordable food to low-income communities, they created an industrial and provident society, a community benefit company that allows for diverse investments from members. The volunteering model, together with the maximum use of recycled fixtures and the minimisation of waste, enables the venture to match and even undercut large competitors on some product lines, without having to rely on low-quality or volume brand suppliers.

A one-member one-vote system means that all members have a say in daily operations. They also get to vote on which products are stocked, which means that Coca-Cola and Cadbury's chocolate can be found alongside independently sourced organic and biodynamic foods. The People's Supermarket does however attempt to source products from local and small-scale providers where possible – for instance, some of its salads come from a nearby community garden, tended by volunteers.

The forging of strong networks with companies and residents enabled more than half of the start-up cost to be covered by donated services and materials – sourced from receivers, a range of corporates and the community. The remainder was a mixture of interest-free loans, charity grants, sweat equity and minimal public sector subsidy – creating a hybrid venture that aims to be a commercial success but uses its profits entirely to benefit the community. Integral to this was a branding strategy that, according to its founders, aimed to establish The People's Supermarket as 'communal, affordable and democratic without appearing too virtuous or elitist'; all branding and labels were designed so that they could be produced in-house.

The shop itself is diversifying: it runs cookery classes; a lunchtime take-away service has started in response to local demand and in order to reduce food waste; and the shop now 'hosts' a florist who was forced out of nearby retail premises after a rent increase. Members have gone on 'crop rescue missions' to farms to collect produce disregarded by larger supermarkets because of size requirements. The venture is also to launch a home-delivery service by bicycle, supported by philanthropic funding.

The venture will create a diverse social return on investment – up-skilling local people, benefiting their household budgets, retaining profits within the area and providing a space where low-income and other residents can mix in the everyday business of volunteering and shopping.

IMPACT

Nearly one year after its launch, The People's Supermarket is breaking even and its membership has been growing steadily. Some of the volunteers – around 60% of whom are local – have started apprenticeship programmes that will enable them to take on increasing responsibilities, often starting from a low skills base. The People's Supermarket now has two full-time employees supported by a welfare-to-work programme, answering to a store manager who is fully funded by a charitable foundation.

KEY LESSONS

RECOGNISING THE PROTAGONISTS

Indirect local authority support

Beyond the initiators themselves, two factors that helped the start-up of The People's Supermarket in this location (previous attempts to establish the project on other sites had failed) were the facilitating role of Camden Council and the supportive ethos of the landowner. Although the council provided only a relatively small direct subsidy, its officers played a crucial role in brokering the agreement by strongly supporting the proposition – recognising that it contributed to their regeneration policy objectives. The landowner, a charitable trust, recognised the valuable community aims of the project, though its decision was in the end a commercial one, based on the project's business case.

PARTICIPATION BEYOND CONSULTATION

A collaborative product

The local engagement model was not one of typical community participation, since occupancy of the premises depended on confidential negotiations over the lease. This made extensive engagement in advance of occupation of the premises difficult. However, once the location had been secured and the concept was introduced into the community, its benefits were clearly articulated to local people. In this case, having a participative product (through volunteering and co-governance) was more important than a participative process.

GENERATING CHANGE THROUGH NETWORKS

Adaptation not replication

The People's Supermarket wants to grow – but as a genuinely localist concept, not as a roll-out franchise. It is therefore about to issue community shares to existing and future members. The founders are committed to helping others across the UK create similar ventures, but based upon entrepreneurial adaptation of the model to meet local needs and opportunities. This, they feel, is crucial to the quality of the local business case, and to the local experience crucial to making the concept a success.

IN CONCLUSION

How can we strengthen a local sense of belonging in our high streets? The People's Supermarket shows how new hybrid ventures can retain wealth in local neighbourhoods and re-imagine the grocery shop as a place where people do not just buy for their daily needs but also enjoy an active stake and daily interaction. Creating such long-term social returns requires not just a new generation of civic enterprise but also a greater availability of mixed mode investment sources.

OTHER EXAMPLES

The Bear Co-op, Todmorden, UK, 1980

...is a health food co-operative shop and café, which encourages food growers to sell directly from the shop, and uses produce from Incredible Edible Todmorden gardens (see case study 12) in its café.

Park Slope Food Coop, New York, USA, 1973

...is a members-only supermarket co-operative; in exchange for voluntary work once every month, members receive 20%-40% discounts on their groceries.

Green Valley Grocer, Slaithwaite, UK, 2009

...is a community-owned co-operative in West Yorkshire that took over a grocer's shop when the previous owners retired; its refurbishment was funded through a community share offer, volunteering and in-kind donations from other businesses.

Top: Rutland Telecom founder David Lewis presents the interchange to the BBC. Bottom: A close-up of the interchange

21

RUTLAND TELECOM

**A COMMUNITY INTERNET PROVIDER
LYDDINGTON, UNITED KINGDOM**

'For rural areas – if they are connected at all – the average [broadband speed] is 3 megabits per second. Will you put up with that? The people of Rutland didn't! The result is that Britain's smallest county has the best broadband. I find this story so inspiring.'

Neelie Kroes, Vice President of the European Commission and European Digital Agenda Commissioner

17 MB / SECOND BROADBAND SPEED IN RUTLAND

8.61 MB / SECOND AVERAGE SPEED ACROSS THE UK

£37,000 START-UP CAPITAL RAISED FROM LOCAL RESIDENTS

25% RESIDENTS SIGNED UP IN FIRST YEAR

BUILDING THE PATHWAY TO LOCAL UTILITIES PROVISION

01 SHARED AWARENESS OF LOCAL DISSATISFACTION THROUGH INFORMAL DISCUSSIONS OVER TIME

02 FUTURE ENTREPRENEUR HAS AWARENESS OF TECHNOLOGICAL / REGULATORY POSSIBILITIES

03 ENTREPRENEUR ORGANISES MEETING IN VILLAGE HALL INVITING LOCAL PEOPLE AND PROVIDING CHAMPAGNE

04 10 MONTHS OF REPEATED PUBLIC MEETINGS AND INFORMAL CONVERSATIONS; FINALLY 40 PRE-REGISTRATIONS OBTAINED AS WELL AS STARTING CAPITAL

05 ROLE OF THIRD-PARTY INFLUENCERS TO 'TRANSLATE' TECH-TALK INTO LANGUAGE THAT VILLAGERS UNDERSTAND AND TRUST

06 SUPPORT FROM PARISH COUNCIL; PLANNING PERMISSION OBTAINED

07 BATTLES WITH LARGE-SCALE PROVIDER OVER TECHNICAL & CONTRACTUAL OBLIGATIONS TOWARDS START-UP VENTURE

08 LAST-MINUTE FUNDRAISING FOR ADDITIONAL CAPITAL BRINGS IN £10,000 IN A SINGLE WEEK

£10K

09 TECHNICAL TRIALS AND PUBLIC OPENING

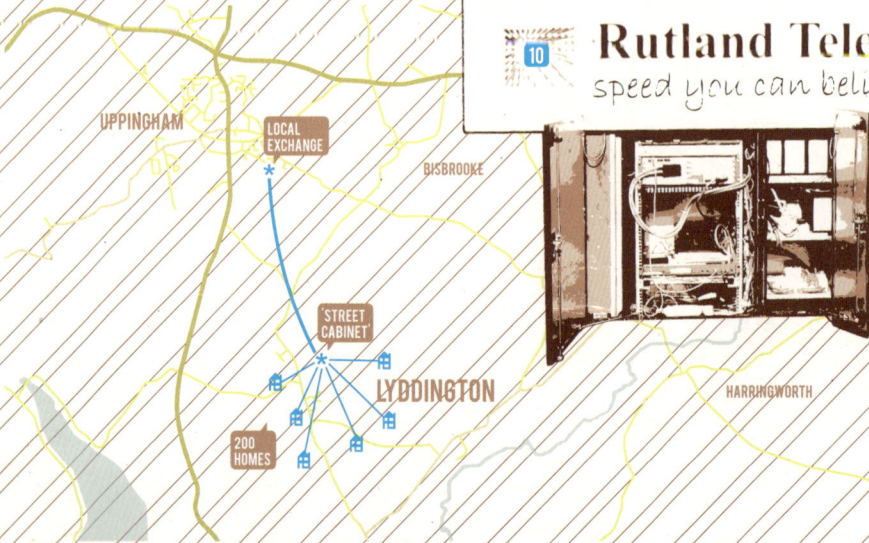

10 Rutland Telecom
speed you can believe in!

UPPINGHAM

LOCAL EXCHANGE

BISBROOKE

'STREET CABINET'

LYDDINGTON

200 HOMES

HARRINGWORTH

THE STORY

If the major utilities companies don't deliver, an alternative is possible: in the rural village of Lyddington in Leicestershire, a partnership between technologically savvy entrepreneurs and the wider community created a broadband infrastructure with average internet speeds far surpassing those of many cities.

Over the past decade, the reluctance of telecoms companies to install next generation broadband networks in sparsely populated areas with insufficient customer-bases has caused a growing digital divide between rural and urban Britain. However, thanks to an ingenious community self-provision enterprise, the residents of Lyddington enjoy incredible internet speeds.

Rutland Telecom was conceived in 2007 by David Lewis and Mark Melluish, who both had experience in the telecoms sector and knew how to use existing legislation to gain access to BT's broadband infrastructure. Using new, but readily available, technology, the firm set up a 'street cabinet' in Lyddington, which works as a mini telephone exchange. This enables Rutland Telecom to provide the village's 200 homes with high-speed internet access through existing lines.

After many conversations with residents working from home, families wishing to shop online and retired people active in UK-wide voluntary work, David Lewis called a meeting in the village hall in June 2008 to assess support for his idea. A minimum of 40 pre-registrations was required (equivalent to a fifth of the households in the village) as well as start-up capital. Over the next 10 months, through a range of formal and informal meetings and helped by influential people in the village communicating the project to other residents, the necessary registrations were obtained and finance raised.

It helped that the village already had a loose group of residents accustomed to working together and an active village hall, and that the initiative was generally perceived as a project for the benefit of the whole community. As a consequence, several people volunteered their time and resources to help the company on its way, bringing in potential investors and subscribers. Those who invested did so not just to get better broadband and a financial return but also to support a positive village project. The parish council was also positive, and planning permission was swiftly obtained.

A series of hurdles in the technical and contractual relation with BT were overcome through reference to Ofcom rules and the persistence and know-how of the founders. The relations built up in the village ensured that a last-minute £10,000 rise in the set-up cost could be dealt with within a week. After several months of trials, the network was officially opened in April 2010 and provides more than 25% of local residents with high-speed internet.

IMPACT

Rutland Telecom is now the fastest internet service provider in the region. Internet speeds are the highest for any rural village in the UK and higher than most major cities. Rutland Telecom has expanded outside Lyddington and is now available to more than half the residents in Rutland, through locally differentiated funding strategies. In some villages, there have been single large investors; in others, capital was raised through a surcharge on the subscription rates. The company is also trying to help similar start-ups across the country and has been approached by more than 200 rural communities interested in setting up their own internet service provider. Following the government's decision to encourage private sector and community-based internet service providers, especially in rural areas, there are plans to develop similar projects as pilots across the UK.

KEY LESSONS

RECOGNISING THE PROTAGONISTS

A local action coalition

Rutland Telecom shows how small communities can be self-reliant and create infrastructure at the most appropriate scale: technologically savvy and highly networked residents working together were able to spot the opportunity and unlock initial support and subsequent investment in the kind of venture that is normally the domain of large companies or the public sector. The original proposition required extensive engagement with residents to overcome scepticism about the local provision of what looks like mass infrastructure. The existing social networks and trust provided fertile ground for the protagonists to succeed largely independent from public sector involvement.

FINANCIAL CO-INVESTMENT

Local investors

The finance for the initial investment was provided by local people. When banks proved unwilling to provide loans for the new venture, the founders turned to the community. All the £37,000 start-up funding was provided by 11 local residents who have a non-voting equity stake and enjoy a 10% return on their investments. In the case of Rutland, the geographical scale of the community was small enough so that no online fundraising platform was needed for this: it happened through informal face-to-face contact.

RECOGNISING WHERE VALUE LIES

Enabling the small

A key hurdle for Rutland Telecom was its need for detailed information about which addresses in a locality are connected to which street cabinet. This data was crucial to work out the cost of supplying areas with new fibre-optic networks, but were held by the large existing provider. Under existing regulatory rules, this information has to be available to all parties on an equal basis; only after Rutland Telecom applied significant pressure, Ofcom stepped into the dispute to enforce this level playing field to the benefit of smaller players.

IN CONCLUSION

How do we create pathways and interfaces for citizens to invest directly in the daily infrastructures they need? In a time when core infrastructure provision is almost invariably seen as a large-scale challenge, Rutland Telecom shows that marrying decentralised technology to a smaller grain of investment can unlock distributed resources for shared projects that benefit the public domain – but also that this may require a regulatory and culture shift.

OTHER EXAMPLES

The Phone Co-op, Chipping Norton, UK, 1998
...is the UK's only telephone co-op; it has 15,000 customers, half of whom are members. Profits are given back to members as dividends or used to fund other environmentally friendly co-operative projects.

The High Line, New York, USA, 2009
...is a linear park on a disused railway elevated in Manhattan's West Side; though operated as a public park by the City of New York, it is largely funded by the Friends of the High Line, a community-based non-profit group that raises money for the project.

OpenIDEO, Palo Alto, USA / London, UK, 2010
...is an online global innovation challenge community founded by the design consultancy IDEO; it crowd-sources ideas for complex social issues from open communities of creative thinkers, through time-limited challenge projects sponsored by public and private partners.

An informal gathering of Southwark Circle members

22

SOUTHWARK CIRCLE

A NEIGHBOURHOOD SOCIAL SUPPORT NETWORK
LONDON, UNITED KINGDOM

'I'm glad that the group of people who have formed Southwark Circle can make a contribution themselves, everyone must feel that they value themselves more. Other organisations, it's as if you've been given something which is good. But Southwark Circle is more like you're doing things with other people because you choose to.'

Carol, Southwark Circle member

£3
SAVINGS FOR
EVERY POUND
INVESTED,
ACCORDING TO
EARLY EVALUATION

700
MEMBERS IN
SOUTHWARK
CIRCLE

250
PEOPLE OVER
50 INVOLVED IN
18-MONTH
CO-DESIGN PROCESS

GENERATING A PEER-TO-PEER EXCHANGE FOR EVERYDAY SERVICES

JOINING THE CIRCLE

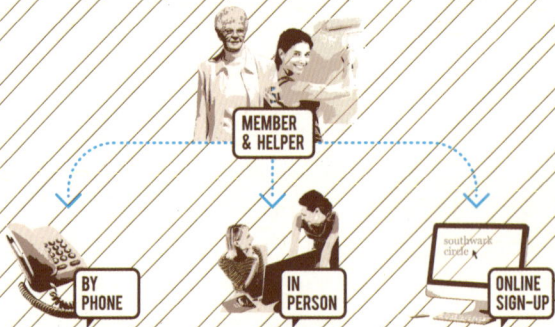

MEMBER & HELPER

BY PHONE

IN PERSON

ONLINE SIGN-UP

TYPES OF EXCHANGE

FINANCIAL EXCHANGE — MEMBERS PURCHASE HELPER TIME

TIME EXCHANGE — HELPERS GIVE TIME, AND THEN BANK IT

SOCIAL EXCHANGE — HELPERS & MEMBERS ENCOURAGED TO MEET

OUTCOMES

FIONA — * CALLS THE HELPLINE

HUGH — BANKS TIME — * HUGH TEACHES MUSIC

SARAH — EARNS A WAGE — PURCHASES HELPER TIME — * HUGH GAINS COMPUTER LITERACY

ANNA — EARNS CREDITS — * CARRIES SHOPPING HOME FOR FIONA

SWAPS CREDITS — * ANNA SWAPS CREDITS FOR MUSIC LESSONS

* HUGH, ANNA, FIONA & SARAH MEET FOR COFFEE

THE STORY

Not all aspects of quality of life and well-being depend on 'big' issues such as health or income. Getting an electrical appliance fixed, learning how to use Skype or picking up the shopping and meeting someone with similar interests make a big difference. The trick is to bring these wants and needs together with the capabilities in the community, and to make it possible for someone who helps with some things to themselves receive help with other needs. That is what Southwark Circle was designed to do: fulfilling everyday needs through a social support network and in the process reducing social isolation in an inner-London borough.

Southwark Circle was the result of a unique partnership between the service design practice Participle, Southwark Council, the Department for Work and Pensions, and Sky that started in September 2007. In order to understand better the community's needs and aspirations, it was developed with the active co-design of more than 250 older people and their families over the course of 18 months, before being launched in May 2009 as a community interest company. News of the launch was spread via local newspapers, word of mouth, and by a temporary stall set up in front of a supermarket to create awareness of the scheme outside existing social networks.

For £10 per year, Southwark residents over the age of 50 can join the Circle, which is mediated via telephone and internet. Membership offers the opportunity to contribute to, and participate in, a lively social calendar, and to buy tokens giving access to the active network of CRB-checked 'Neighbourhood Helpers'. Helpers may be Circle members who also volunteer, or non-members who are paid the London living wage for their time. Each token is equivalent to about an hour's work and the help provided ranges from gardening and cleaning to computer lessons and general advice. The scheme thereby caters to otherwise unmet needs of the community, adding to the public service offer and strengthening local social networks. Members who are struggling with small everyday problems can get them fixed without having to pay large sums to commercial providers or turn to relatives or social services. Helpers can choose to be either voluntary or paid, which enables retired or unemployed people as well as active professionals to use their skills in a productive and appreciated manner.

The monthly member calendar is composed of many events that are suggested or hosted by members and helpers. It also features discounts on products and services. The calendar is a 'continuation of life' for many members, offering opportunities to meet people, learn new skills and share their interests. Helpers are also encouraged to socialise whilst working and many have already created long-lasting professional relationships and friendships.

Southwark Circle has been designed as a social enterprise that can be fully self-sufficient by its third year as it reaches its target of 2,000 members. At this point, Southwark Council will withdraw its funding and the Circle will be financed solely through membership fees, bookings and private donations. In its first year, it beat growth targets by 15%; it continues to grow both in the borough and across the country as an innovative model.

IMPACT

After a year, Southwark Circle has 700 members, and has been growing faster than expected. Although the financial benefits are still to be proven, early evidence suggests that for every pound invested, Southwark Council will save three pounds. This is achieved by reducing the day-to-day services that the council has to provide, through helping residents gain employment and by improving members' well-being, thereby reducing GP visits. Now that early success is becoming evident, Southwark Circle's infrastructure and organisational structure can be replicated in other areas. New schemes have already started in Suffolk and Hammersmith & Fulham. The model allows for customisation in accordance with local needs and resources. In Suffolk, for example, the scheme has been designed to incorporate car sharing possibilities, as there is a great need for transport solutions in this rural area.

KEY LESSONS

PARTICIPATION BEYOND CONSULTATION

User-led service design

One of the primary factors behind the Circle's success is the fact that it was created with local residents. This has allowed the scheme to provide services that are tailored to local needs and has ultimately helped boost the project's popularity and usage. Many services are, moreover, provided by people from the neighbourhood: about a third of the helpers are also members, thus creating a user co-production model. The quality of the user interface is crucial for this model to succeed. In this case that has been achieved through the co-development of an easy-access, low-barriers platform combining online and offline communication.

GENERATING CHANGE THROUGH NETWORKS

Connected entrepreneurs

Southwark Circle was initiated by Participle's internationally recognised social innovation experts, who were able to organise significant support from across the public sector both locally and nationally. Their reputation encouraged Southwark Council to participate in the project even when its benefits were yet unproven, and despite its reliance on qualitative metrics and evaluation types beyond those normally employed in the public sector. Equally, their involvement has enabled relatively rapid scaling beyond the original pilot towards a series of other locations.

RE-USING EXISTING ASSETS

Unleashing people's strengths

Fundamentally, Southwark Circle is based on the premise that many of the everyday social needs in an urban neighbourhood could be met by the time, skills and energy of others nearby. The fact that this does not normally happen could be perceived as a gap in the market which the venture aims to fill through an easy-access network that brings both together. The Circle strengthens a sense of neighbourhood interdependency by both enabling and celebrating the favours that people can offer each other, in a way that prevents people from becoming more dependent on mainstream services.

IN CONCLUSION

How do we create platforms and institutions that help people support each other, and become more self-reliant through mutual interdependence? Southwark Circle focuses on what people can offer one another and unlocks frequently ignored resources for often unmet needs. This investment is essential across our neighbourhoods: it allows us to strengthen the unseen virtual and social networks that will enable our physical places to prosper and be more resilient.

OTHER EXAMPLES

The Good Gym, London, UK, 2008
...grew out of its founders' frustration with the lack of social purpose in regular fitness clubs and was launched at Social Innovation Camp; it pairs 'runners' with tasks for isolated less-mobile people in their area, making volunteering easy and fun, and connecting people.

School of Everything, UK, 2006
...is an online platform that is reversing the top-down approach to learning by enabling would-be learners in any topic to connect with would-be teachers in their local area.

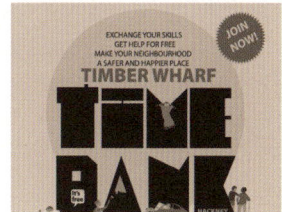

Timber Wharf Time Bank, London, UK, 2009
...is a free online skills exchange network in Hackney, where local residents can help others in return for 'time credit' that they can swap to receive help from others.

Inside Studio Hergebruik, the re-occupied ground floor of a vacant 1960s office block

23

STUDIO HERGEBRUIK

A MEANWHILE STUDIO FOR RE-USE DESIGNERS
ROTTERDAM, THE NETHERLANDS

'It's a place that inspires and challenges people so they can get from nice ideas to real projects. It helped me connect to manufacturing companies that I would have found difficult to get access to, and it gave me an international platform to work with other designers working with 'trash' ... it's a real spider in a web of possibilities.'

Esther Derkx, a designer specialising in re-using discarded crockery and PVC mesh material

20,000
VISITORS & 125 WORKSHOPS IN 2010 AFTER BUILDING WAS EMPTY FOR 7 YEARS

80
DESIGNERS IN THE NETWORK

€0
PUBLIC SUBSIDY

SHOWING, CONNECTING, ENABLING & FINANCING A NEXT GENERATION OF DESIGNERS

SHOWROOM FOR START-UP DESIGNERS

INTERNATIONAL KNOWLEDGE NETWORK

SHARED WORKSHOP AND EVENT SPACE

SEED INVESTMENT IN NEW VENTURES AND IDEAS

CEILING LEFT AS FOUND UPON RE-OCCUPATION OF THE BUILDING

BEHIND THESE CURTAINS MADE FROM RECYCLED MESH-ADVERTISING CANVAS IS AN OPEN-PLAN WORKSHOP & CO-WORKING SPACE

ADDITIONAL EXHIBITION & EVENT SPACE UPSTAIRS

PUBLIC WORKSHOPS TAKE PLACE ON THE PAVEMENT IN SUMMER

GROUND FLOOR SHOWROOM & EVENT SPACE

RECYCLED PRODUCTS INCLUDING VASES MADE FROM BROKEN CERAMICS & CHAIRS FROM CAR TYRES

LAMP MADE FROM DISCARDED LABORATORY TEST BOTTLES

CHANDELIER MADE FROM MULTIPLE DISCARDED CHANDELIERS

SECOND-HAND CROCKERY WITH NEW DECORATION

TABLE MADE OF RECOVERED WOOD FROM DEMOLISHED ROTTERDAM HOUSES

FURNITURE MADE FROM RECYCLED BOOKS

THE STORY

Studio Hergebruik (Re-use Studio) is a meeting place, a knowledge centre and a platform for creativity in the growing re-use economy. It displays and sells work by product designers and artists from all creative disciplines that focus on re-use and recycling of materials or concepts. Numerous functions are combined; besides a shop, documentation centre, exhibition space, gallery and conference room, it also offers workspaces for educational activities.

The Re-use Studio was started in the Netherlands in 2005 by Jan de Haas, a retired entrepreneur, after an informal conversation with the owners of an empty 1960s office building opposite Rotterdam's City Hall. Aware that the growing community of designers and artists working with recycled materials needed better access to the market, he suggested he could find a use for at least part of the building, which had been empty for more than six years. A space in the centre of the city would enable designers to make their presence known, sell their products, and develop ideas and creations further.

The Re-use Studio now occupies a large part of the ground and first floors of the building. Realising that the slack property market in the city provided few alternatives, the landowners gave De Haas the space for two years, without a formal business plan or contract, and at a nominal rent.

From an empty ground floor, the Re-use Studio has become an active part of the city's innovation, education and retail offer, supporting around 80 designers in different ways, and working with many secondary and higher education institutions. The studio offers facilities for prototyping and product development, and all areas are open to the public. One of its most important goals is to inspire people – both designers and the general public – and to bring them together around a platform from which to exchange knowledge. The studio therefore also organises lectures and masterclasses, and offers internships, educational workshops and exhibition spaces to Dutch and international art academies, universities and art schools, as well as team-building events for companies. Its main income streams are the sale of products and educational activities; these enable the studio to invest seed capital in the work of starting designers.

The building's lease is based on an 'anti-squatting' licence through which landlords rent out property at low rates while they decide what to do with it in the longer term. In practice, this helps to provide low-rent solutions to many budding businesses. Other tenants in the building include an architecture practice that specialises in reusing materials, thereby creating a mini-cluster of like-minded people.

IMPACT

Although 'meanwhile' projects are widely used throughout the Netherlands as anti-squatting measure, the practice had not previously been seen as a deliberate regeneration strategy. This changed with the success of Studio Hergebruik and other temporary ventures in empty ground floors, which had visible impact in a city that suffers from a weak property market. In 2008 the City of Rotterdam created a policy encouraging such collaborations by relaxing zoning regulations and other rules for landowners opening up vacant buildings for creative uses, thus lowering the regulatory threshold for re-occupation. Publicly owned assets are also used to this end. The policy of open-endedness based on bottom-up creativity has become more and more embedded as an economic development mechanism.

KEY LESSONS

RECOGNISING THE PROTAGONISTS

Networking a budding sector

The founder's personal contacts spanned the creative and the property sector, enabling him to connect needs and opportunities on both sides. With no pressure to 'deliver' a ready-made concept, he developed a venture that could evolve, without submitting a formal business plan. His main aim was to support the fledgling re-make community by helping them share experiences and know-how, and support each other's design and production processes. Selling products was at first a secondary element, but grew into a main income stream as it gave them access to the market. Thus the Studio generates direct economic as well as creative benefit for its members; its education activities and its ability to provide small-scale capital investments further strengthens the ability of the designers to scale up their activities.

RE-USING EXISTING ASSETS

Rethinking waste and vacancy

The proposition is geared around the idea that the re-use of materials and spaces is not just an environmental imperative but also a creative challenge that can reach a surprisingly wide audience. Moreover, whilst Rotterdam's many empty buildings had for a long time been seen as indicative of the city's economic problems, they are now increasingly recognised as an opportunity for start-up entrepreneurs, distinguishing the city from other parts of the Netherlands where business space can be harder to find. The easy availability of space at low rents and with flexible contracts has contributed to Rotterdam's reputation for creative entrepreneurship.

THE EXPERIENCE OF PLACE

Telling the story

The Studio is a deliberately multifunctional space, with a clear message to the public: ReUse – ReThink – ReSearch – ReConsider – ReMake. It portrays itself both as a movement with a purpose and as a proposition that appeals to a discerning community of designers and ethical consumers. The double-height Modernist space and the intensity of the experience work together to create what De Haas calls a 'buzz' and a 'playground' – where quality is key to convince the public that this is not a marginal community of do-gooders but an attractive way of living and doing.

IN CONCLUSION

How do we create a new purpose for vacant spaces and sites that have lost their original use? Ironically, 'meanwhile' projects are most valuable if we recognise that they need to be part of a more permanent strategic policy approach that supports the full diversity of talent in our cities to emerge and flourish. Thus 'meanwhile' experiments help us understand what fertile ground for the future civic economy looks like.

OTHER EXAMPLES

L'Hub, Milan, Italy, 2009
...is a collective craft space where the public can learn about and experiment with textiles and handcrafts, supported by design and upcycling workshops led by artisans.

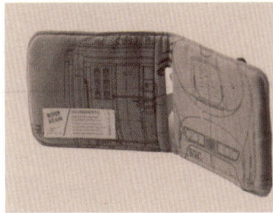

Worn Again, London, UK, 2005
...is an eco-fashion company that works with companies to upcycle discarded materials into clothes and accessories, and provides consultancy to large firms on dealing with excess fabric.

The Chocolate Factory, London, UK, 1996
...is a hub for more than 200 artists and creative practitioners, housed in a former confectionery factory, offering studios and exhibition spaces and business support.

Customers outside the recently expanded TCHO tasting room at the San Francisco factory

24

TCHO

A PARTICIPATIVE 'DOWNTOWN' CHOCOLATE MANUFACTURER
SAN FRANCISCO, UNITED STATES

'The presence of TCHO in Downtown San Francisco is beneficial on several levels. The quality and ethics of TCHO chocolates support San Francisco's leadership in culinary arts and sustainability. And its products extend a little bit of the San Francisco experience to customers wherever it is consumed.'

Laurie Armstrong, San Francisco Convention and Tourism Bureau

2,800	3	10,000
SQUARE METRE DOWNTOWN FACTORY	FLAVOR LABS ESTABLISHED IN 3 SUPPLIER COUNTRIES	MEMBERS OF ONLINE TASTERS CIRCLE

ORGANISING A COLLABORATIVE FOOD PRODUCTION CHAIN

2005   2006   2007   2008   2009   2010   2011

05 4 YEARS OF BETA-TESTING GROWS A STRONG PRODUCT & PRE-LAUNCH COMMUNITY

DOWNTOWN LOCATION EMBEDS PRODUCTION INTO THE LIFE OF THE CITY

DOWNTOWN FACTORY

STORE

CONSUMERS

MICRO-INVESTORS
INITIAL INVESTMENT BY FRIENDS & FAMILY WHO ALSO TEST THE PRODUCT. A LARGE NUMBER OF SMALL INVESTORS ENABLES INDEPENDENCE FROM IMPATIENT VENTURE CAPITAL FUNDING

TCHO CHOCOLATE

TASTING ROOM
COMBINED FACTORY, SHOP AND TASTING ROOM GENERATES CUSTOMER FEEDBACK

01

BETA-TESTERS
02 STRONG ONLINE MEMBERSHIP OF TASTERS REFINE THE PRODUCT & BUILD LOYAL FOLLOWING

FLAVOR LAB

GROWERS
GROWERS PARTICIPATE & ADD VALUE – LEADING TO AWARDS WON FOR TASTE AND QUALITY

1ST

03

04 FLAVOR LABS DEPLOYED TO SUPPLIER COUNTRIES ENABLING GROWERS TO TASTE THEIR CHOCOLATE FOR THE FIRST TIME

06

07

08

MICRO-FINANCE

CROWD-SOURCED CO-DEVELOPMENT

MAKING GLOBAL LINKAGES TRANSPARENT

INNOVATIVE SUPPLY CHAIN

COLLABORATIVE BRAND

STRONG IDENTITY LOCAL PRESENCE

PARTICIPATIVE PRODUCT

THE STORY

A civic economy approach to manufacturing starts with changing how
raw material inputs are sourced,
but reaches all the way to shift the
relation between the consumer and
production process. From an inner-
city food production facility with an
open door to the public, San Francisco chocolate manufacturer TCHO
has done both, thereby changing the
entire production chain of its business. Furthermore, the company
sees this approach as part of its very
DNA, rather than a CSR add-on.

TCHO is the only chocolate company to manufacture
chocolate in San Francisco since 1967. The company was
created in 2005 by Timothy Childs, a NASA researcher,
and Karl Bittong, a chocolate industry veteran. A considerable part of the start-up finance was raised by friends
and family, who received equity in the firm. This funding
model allowed the company to be relatively independent
of commercial interests during the supply chain development process and to experiment with a combination of
state-of-the-art technology and traditional production
equipment – including recycled dhal cookers.

TCHO then invited friends, family and investors to test
the beta-versions of four flavours of chocolate, and continued this approach using social media: samples were
sent out to 'beta-testers' through an online platform.
Over the course of several years, its chocolate has been
continuously co-developed and improved, to attain top
quality standards. After this thorough start-up and testing period, TCHO eventually started selling its chocolate
in 2009.

An integral element of this open relation with the public
is the company's location: instead of working from an
isolated business park, TCHO has located its 2,800 sq m
factory on Pier 17, a prominent site in downtown San
Francisco, deliberately chosen because of its high acces-
sibility to the public. Combined with a 'tasting room' and
shop – which were recently expanded – the factory aims
to make the production process as transparent as possible. The City of San Francisco played a facilitating role,
enabling permits and permissions once they realised the
potential of this venture to change the mix of activities
on the waterfront.

Changing the supply chain is another part of TCHO's
approach: not only does it comply with fair trade price
standards but through its pioneering TCHOSource programme it has invested heavily in up-skilling its cocoa
suppliers. It has opened 'Flavor Labs' in supplier countries, helping farmers to understand the post-harvest
production process and taste chocolate made from the
beans they have grown – often for the very first time. This
helps them to educate other farmers, creating a virtuous
open-source cycle where suppliers upgrade their skills
and production processes, and obtain a much better price
on the general market.

By rethinking the way chocolate manufacturing takes
place and creating platforms for collaboration both at
source and for the end-product, TCHO has not only been
able to produce substantially better chocolate but has
also opened up the possibility for farmers to move up the
value chain.

IMPACT

Less than three years from its first sales, the company is already a commercial success. It serves most of the US West Coast, its products are sold in major cities in Europe and Japan, and the company is planning to expand further. TCHOSource and the Flavor Lab approach have led to substantial gains for cacao farmers and improved the quality of TCHO's raw materials. Two TCHO suppliers came first and third in the 2008 National Cocoa Competition in Peru – one of them had not even taken part before. More than 10,000 people have signed up as members of its online Tasters Circle. The tasting room has been significantly expanded, allowing visitors an even closer look at the production process, and there are plans for collaboration with a new next-door neighbour, the Exploratorium science museum, on food and science topics.

KEY LESSONS

PARTICIPATION BEYOND CONSULTATION

Open-source product development

Many innovative product branding strategies go beyond market research to allow for customisation and thus create a 'collaborative brand' – TCHO went further and put its raw input suppliers at the heart of the collaboration. Therefore they created the Flavor Labs, a local platform for product innovation at source that is also a way of building capabilities and co-developing a better product. Instead of focusing on cost reduction alone, this is a workforce investment approach; knowledge-transfer to producers leads to improvement in quality, which eventually leads to cost savings, by removing the need to continuously monitor and intervene in the production process.

THE EXPERIENCE OF PLACE

Uniting production and consumption

The downtown harbour-front location is an integral part of TCHO's business model. It is worth the high rent because it reduces the psychological and actual distance between producers and consumers, and makes evident the company's ambition to become a 'new American manufacturer' of chocolate. TCHO sees participation as integral to its market, not just to create a sensory culinary experience for visitors but because ethical transparency is crucial to building credibility and trust. Locating production facilities in the heart of the city changes the city centre itself, as it maintains a diversity of functions and experiences beyond a purely retail and services landscape.

GENERATING CHANGE THROUGH NETWORKS

An open-source training model

Just as social networks were crucial to TCHO's start-up – its founders had connections to the tech magazine Wired and could link into a wide group of investors and supporters – the company also uses networks to spread its benefits. The Flavor Lab programme is scalable, as up-skilled farmers can train others, which helps to create a cost-efficient training model. The Flavor Lab is an open-source model that TCHO hopes other producers will adopt, thereby making the continued improvement of cacao quality a standard industry practice.

IN CONCLUSION

What could a new fusion of production and consumption look like in the heart of our towns and cities? TCHO shows that a new breed of manufacturing companies can benefit from locating themselves not on any business park but right within the existing built fabric. Based on ethical principles and wide participation through social networks, they generate jobs and create benefits across the production chain – and show that separating land uses often makes no sense.

OTHER EXAMPLES

Osted Dairy, Osted, Denmark, 1997

...is a dairy and cheese shop housed in a former petrol station, where the public can not only see the entire production process through large windows but also step inside the former car wash space to talk to the staff.

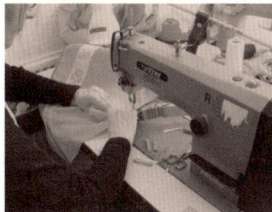

Midshires Clothing Factory, Kettering, UK, 2010

...is a worker-owned clothing co-operative that manufactures healthcare uniforms, bags, aprons and high-visibility clothing, based in a 19th-century school building in a mixed-use neighbourhood.

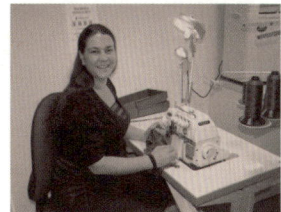

Whomadeyourpants?, Southampton, UK, 2008

...is a worker co-operative that makes ethical underwear, and provides training, jobs and socialising opportunities for marginalised, mainly refugee, women living in inner-city Southampton.

A semi-private courtyard in the French Quarter, Tübingen

25

TÜBINGEN USER-LED HOUSING

A SELF-COMMISSIONED NEIGHBOURHOOD
TÜBINGEN, GERMANY

'A very different way of going about this project allowed us to create a viable housing market in what was a stigmatised area.'

Cord Soehlke, former project director, Tübingen-Südstadt French Quarter

10-20%	6,000	1
CHEAPER THAN CONVENTIONAL HOUSING	RESIDENTS ACROSS TWO NEIGHBOURHOODS	CONTRACT GUIDE DETAILING THE PROCESS TO PROSPECTIVE SELF-COMMISSIONERS

LEADING THE WAY TO A DIFFERENT HOUSING APPROACH

1991	1994	1995	1996	1999	2011

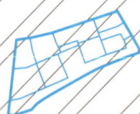     

THE IDEA

DESIRE TO 'DO A DIFFERENT TYPE OF URBANISM'

THE OWNERSHIP DIMENSION

ASSEMBLES & SUB-DIVIDES THE LAND

THE SPATIAL FRAMEWORK

CREATES A LOOSE, PLOT-WISE MASTERPLAN FOR APARTMENT BLOCKS

THE FIRST INVITATION

GIVES OUT THREE PLOTS TO INITIAL BAUGRUPPEN AS PROOF-OF-CONCEPT TEST ALLOWING FIRST GROUPS OF PIONEERS TO JOIN PROCESS

THE METRICS

AGREES TO SELL FOR LESS THAN MAXIMUM VALUE, INSTEAD USING QUALITY OF PROPOSAL AS KEY CRITERIA ENABLING WIDER PARTICIPATION

THE RESULT

NOW 130 BAUGRUPPEN

PARTNERSHIP WITH UNIVERSITY URBANISTS

FINANCIAL INFRASTRUCTURE

ENGAGES THE MORTGAGE INDUSTRY TO PROVIDE INNOVATIVE AND COLLECTIVE FINANCE ARRANGEMENTS

CREATING AN EASY PATHWAY

CREATES CONTRACT GUIDE TO HELP POTENTIAL SELF-BUILDERS UNDERSTAND THE PROCESS, ENABLING WIDER PARTICIPATION

CREATION OF ASPIRATIONAL VISION

THE ENABLING

CREATES PREFERENTIAL ARRANGEMENT TO ENCOURAGE BAUGRUPPEN OVER STANDARD DEVELOPERS

CITY POLICY-MAKERS	CITY URBAN DESIGNERS	PIONEER SELF-COMMISSIONERS	CITY AS BROKER	CITY AS ENABLER	CRITICAL MASS OF SELF-COMMISSIONERS

THE STORY

A former army barracks area in a German city has been regenerated as a diverse urban neighbourhood, thanks to an experimental process that gave future residents precedence over large developers in commissioning new apartments.

The City of Tübingen acted out of a desire to rethink the development of new neighbourhoods, to make them less monotonous and instead form more vibrant communities. Given weak market demand for the 65-hectare site, which had a negative image resulting from its former use as a French military base, a business-as-usual approach carried significant risk. In 1996, the municipality therefore decided to play a big role in the redevelopment process, using its landownership to create a different housing provision model.

An innovative master plan was created for the Südstadt French Quarter. Instead of giving out large blocks to single developers, it would allow individual apartment buildings of four to eight storeys to be developed plot by plot. Three of the first plots were given over to 'Baugruppen', building partnerships of 5-30 households that would commission the design and construction of their future homes (and then be disbanded upon completion of a project).

The success of this pilot showed that the experimental process could compete with commercial housing. The master plan was revised, to specify that resident-led partnerships were to be given preference over commercial developers in most instances. A legal and financial guidance document was drawn up, to support would-be residents. The municipality also played a brokering role in convincing initially sceptical banks to provide mortgages to the Baugruppen members, though the track record of early success showed that the proposition was less risky than feared. Nevertheless, the project required relatively intensive staffing – a team of four to five full-time people – throughout the start-up and delivery phase. The master plan left considerable flexibility as to the architectural style and density of individual building projects, stipulating only that ground floors were to be kept for non-residential use and that courtyards within the blocks were to be collective space. The collective decision-making process of individual 'building partnerships' led to a diversity in built form as well as content, creating a wide range of housing types in response to user needs, as well as workspaces and shared amenities.

The project was an invitation to the public to procure their homes through collaboration. The municipality decided not to seek the highest return on its land, instead selecting development proposals on the basis of a series of quality criteria such as the planned mix of housing types, the accommodation of other uses, demographic diversity, and financial robustness of the Baugruppen. Together with the removal of private developer profit margins, this enabled the housing to be affordable. Costs were also kept down by allowing groups to build at high density if they so desired, and to contribute their own labour to the construction process. The combination of urban design guidance and deep resident involvement in the design process created a remarkably high-quality outcome: the Baugruppen proved to be creative and demanding clients, and the result was a wide range of apartment styles with high energy-efficiency standards.

IMPACT

The Tübingen-Südstadt French Quarter has gained wide recognition both in Germany and abroad as an economic model and a way of creating an urban quarter with a distinctive character within a relatively short time span. From the initial three Baugruppen, the number of these partnerships has grown to over 130. The area has become known for its diverse architecture, engaging public realm and strong community. A relatively large degree of socio-economic mix has been achieved, in particular by allowing lower-income building groups to build at high densities, though their engagement also relied on federal housing subsidies. Though new at the time, the Baugruppen concept is increasingly being adopted in other municipalities throughout Germany.

KEY LESSONS

RECOGNISING THE PROTAGONISTS

Public sector as local market-maker

The Tübingen municipality acted as a civic entrepreneur: making the development happen not through subsidies but through a brokering role. This consisted of: assembling and sub-dividing the site; creating a master plan to set out the core spatial and use parameters; agreeing to sell sites at an 'area average' price prioritising quality criteria rather than the highest possible price; setting a preferential right of purchase for building partnerships over private developers; supporting the Baugruppen with practical advice and support, including a 'contract guide' with examples of legal, financial and construction management contracts; proactively engaging mortgage lenders to facilitate the testing of a new product and process in a risk-averse sector.

PARTICIPATION BEYOND CONSULTATION

An invitation to co-produce

The market-making process prepared the ground for co-production, which was further enabled by the master plan for the area; this created a flexible protocol that set out minimum guidelines but refrained from being overly restrictive. The master plan enabled a wide range of prospective building partnerships to understand the future feel of the area, by guaranteeing the quality of the public realm and creating a degree of coherence within a diverse end product. Crucially, the guidelines took a flexible line on site size, building height and rear building line, allowing for higher density projects to enable affordability.

RECOGNISING WHERE VALUE LIES

Beyond initial financial return

The municipality deliberately decided not just to enable self-commissioning but to actively prefer self-commissioning over developer-led house building, because of its wish to create an area with a different urban character, based on people's participation. Thus, different metrics were introduced in the process, enabling very different outcomes. Integral to this was the decision not to seek the highest possible price for each site, to maintain affordability. The high quality of the development has lifted property values in what was initially an area of low demand, thus generating a better return on financial investment as well.

IN CONCLUSION

How do we enable people to play a bigger part in creating the homes they will inhabit? A civic economy in the housing sector needs to be supported by a purposeful public sector, creating a market within which local people and businesses can take the initiative together. Creating this framework for small-scale entrepreneurship is equally relevant in other sectors, from maintaining public space to improving social care.

OTHER EXAMPLES

Diggers Self Build, Brighton, UK, 1996
...is a 'self-build for rent' eco-housing project, managed through a tenants co-operative, where the residents were strongly involved in the design and actual construction of the project, although they do not actually own the homes.

Springhill Co-housing, Stroud, UK, 2000
...was the first new-build co-housing scheme to be completed in the UK, and houses around 75 people in a highly eco-friendly and fully pedestrianised develop-ment that includes a communal kitchen and three-storey tree hut.

Nieuw Leyden, Leiden, The Netherlands, 2007
...is a high-density residential project in the centre of Leiden, supported by the municipality and a housing association, where more than half of around 800 homes are built through self-commissioning.

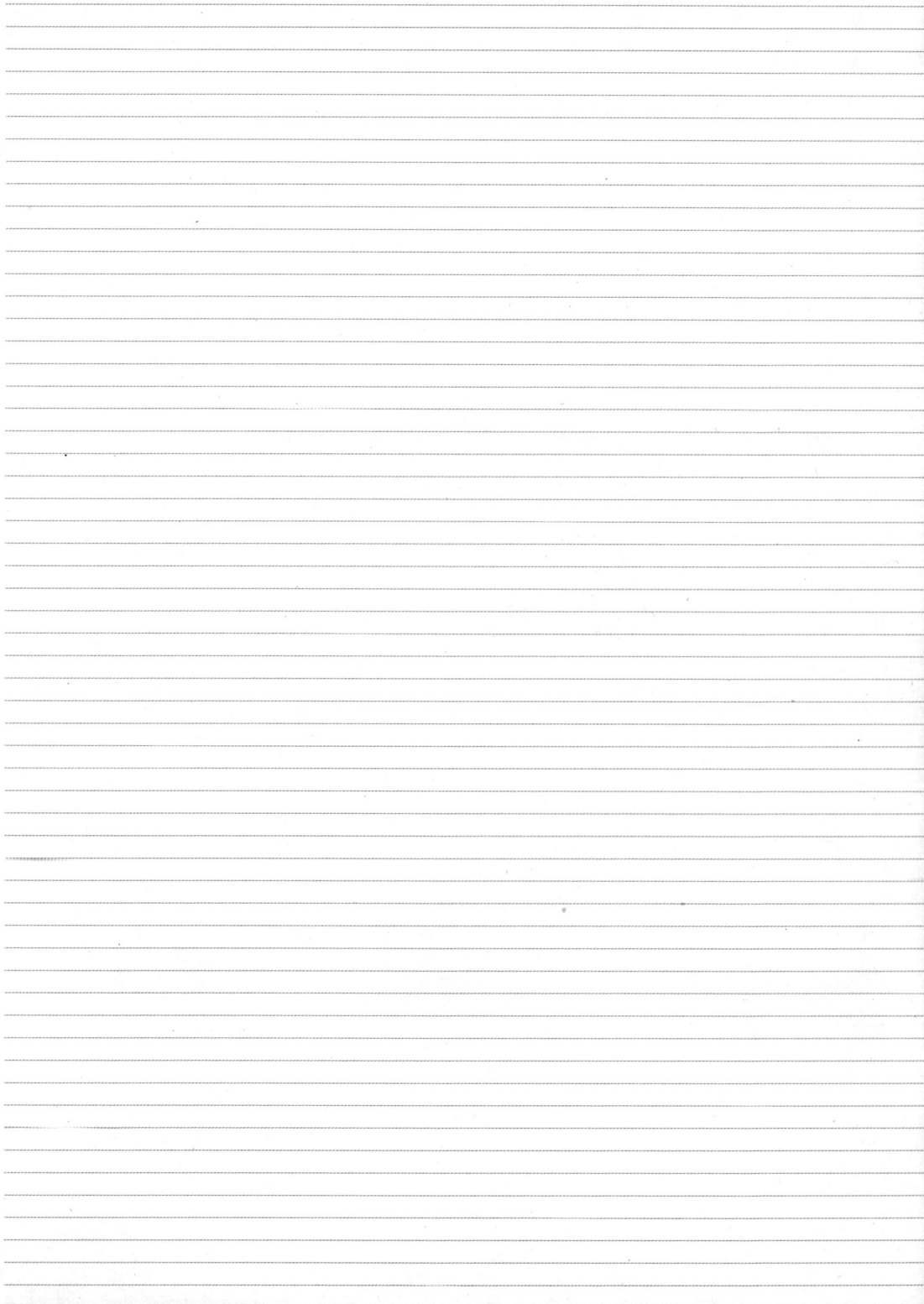

CONCLUSION

1 - See, for a good summary of key figures: Shanmugalingam, C., Graham, J., Tucker, S. and Mulgan, G. (2011) 'Growing Social Ventures - The Role of Intermediaries and Investors: Who They Are, What They Do, and What They Could Become.' London: Young Foundation & NESTA. and Murray, R. (2009) 'Danger and Opportunity – Crisis and the New Social Economy.' London: Young Foundation & NESTA.

LESSONS LEARNED

This book celebrates the civic economy because we believe that it will become an increasingly powerful force for positive change benefiting people and places in the UK. The 25 inspirational stories in this compendium have strengthened not just the economy of their localities but also the quality of the shared public domain and the very fabric of society – in ways that neither the state nor the market have been able to achieve on their own.

They add a new dimension to continuing discussions about both the 'Big Society' and 'StartUp Britain'. The civic enterprises explored in this book show how by linking the two, we can enrich the ongoing debate about growing and re-balancing the economies of places across the UK.

Reflecting on the amazing things achieved by both the 25 trailblazers described in this book and the wide range of other examples we show, six key messages emerge:

The civic economy is re-emerging in a new form as a vital and growing force for social, economic and environmental progress.

In the introduction, we highlighted the technological, cultural and organisational trends that are changing the fabric of our economy and society. These changes are combining with deep-rooted traditions of entrepreneurship, community activism and social enterprise. What results is an emerging set of shifts in behaviour that cut across the public, private and third sector. The size of the civic economy itself is hard to quantify precisely because of its cross-sector nature – but measures such as the size of the social enterprise sector and investment in ethical funds and start-ups are all showing significant growth [1]. Many point to the late 19th and early 20th centuries as the great era of civic pride and vibrancy in the UK – a period of incredible institutional innovation that shaped our towns and cities, their economy, and society as a whole. We now need to recognise that we have entered a new period of similarly deep change in the institutions that underpin our economy and the places we inhabit.

Civic entrepreneurship can actively contribute to increasing the resilience, prosperity and well-being of people, places and communities.

Civic entrepreneurs are achieving change by using collaborative and open-ended approaches to solving some of our most complex societal problems, seeding new ideas and attracting diverse collaborators to shape their propositions. They make innovative use of new technology, innovative finance and wider social networks. They enable better use of undervalued resources whether physical or social. Most importantly, the ventures they create are deeply multi-faceted ventures, demonstrating a range of linked social, economic and environmental outcomes. If their approach were adopted on a wider scale, the outcome would be an economy that is more democratic; locally rooted yet globally networked; richer in opportunities not just for economic growth but also for social development; and pluralist, as it invites multiple forms of investment and widens the scope of players in local economies.

Localities – cities, towns, neighbourhoods and villages – are the focus for the new civic economy.

Recent policy shifts have made it unambiguously clear: it is local places and local people – whether in the public, private or third sector – that must create the trajectories towards renewed, sustainable prosperity that we need. The case studies here give potent examples of the kind of opportunities this could entail in practice. We all need to understand how the examples highlighted in this book relate to local needs and opportunities and how we can enable similar opportunities elsewhere.

Enabling the growth of the civic economy will require different ways of thinking and doing across the public, private and third sector.

The examples in this book cover a wide spectrum: this is an economy that is driven by the purpose and energy of a highly diverse range of protagonists and participants. This means that no single actor – whether the government, local public agencies, or the private or third sector – can on its own create the conditions for the civic entrepreneurs to emerge and flourish. But they all have a role to play in creating fertile ground.

The role of the public sector will often be to provide 'servant leadership' – based upon principles such as intricate awareness of what goes on locally; devolution of decision-making power downwards within their organisations and places; the building of communities of practice; and stewardship over time. This is by no means easy: it requires leaders in localities not just to recognise the latent opportunities and capabilities of people and places but also to re-combine these and bring together innovative ways of, for example, brokering, co-producing, financing, commissioning and measuring success. Fertile ground exists where such disparate elements are stitched together with a real clarity of purpose.

Equally, many within the private sector already understand the benefits of going beyond corporate social responsibility (CSR), embedding social and environmental value agendas at the heart of their business. The case studies hint at the enormous opportunities for those companies that have been able to build the kind of collaborations that turn them into civic enterprises.

The third sector – in all its diversity, from established organisations to citizens working together on an ad-hoc basis – is evidently a hotbed for civic entrepreneurialism. The lessons in this book show ways in which their dynamism can be supported through addressing the arrangements that govern space, procurement and market regulation – thus building the new institutional compact we need to create a more civic economy overall.

Successfully building the civic economy requires us to build bridges between the massive and the micro.

Across these sectors, the challenge is primarily one of scale – one could call it the interface between the 'massive' and the 'micro'. Civic entrepreneurs are opening up pathways for change that enable large-scale organisations or issues to be addressed through small-scale initiative, generating a distributed capacity to invest, create, improve, challenge, learn and innovate. Advances in technology have played an important role in enabling this – but what we now need is institutional change to mirror this: a wider culture shift is needed for the massive and the micro truly to interact – whether in user-led service design, public sector procurement, private-community partnerships or self-provision of utilities. The wealth of good practice in this book is therefore evidence both of where this already happens but also of where additional support is needed.

We must develop a better understanding of the civic economy - and act on it.

Different ways to foster fertile ground are deeply interdependent: this is not a menu of options but an integrated approach. We must start with a better understanding of how the civic economy operates. After all, the civic economy behaves differently from an economy dominated by either the corporate or public sector as we know it.

In the remainder of this conclusion, we outline eight crucial behaviours of the civic economy, and group our recommendations accordingly.

In sum:

A. The civic economy is being built by protagonists who are led by their passion, purpose and personal commitment – and whose key asset is their social networks and trust they hold.

B. The civic economy is based upon inviting participation from the public at large – which goes far beyond mere consultation, to create frameworks for a type of co-production and co-investment that builds deep democratic belonging.

C. The civic economy is built using an increasing diversity of finance sources as well as the investment of a range of other 'currencies' – people's time, trust, and social networks.

D. The civic economy is emerging from recognising and re-combining the latent capacity of dormant or under-used physical assets, human capabilities and aspirations.

E. The civic economy is focused on generating a holistic experience of place – creating places that tell stories about their purpose, often surprising and delighting users and helping to generate open conditions for people's participation and collaboration.

F. The civic economy although purpose-driven, is being built not through strategic planning but through open-ended, agile, incremental and iterative practices – based on starting small and growing in response to evolving needs and opportunities.

G. The civic economy is not just deeply local but also intricately linked to change-makers elsewhere – growing through networks and adaptation rather than through replication.

H. The civic economy is based on delivering a plurality of values and outcomes – which need to be acknowledged and taken into account in formulating the objectives and metrics of new policy, projects and procurement.

A. RECOGNISING THE PROTAGONISTS: CIVIC ENTREPRENEURS

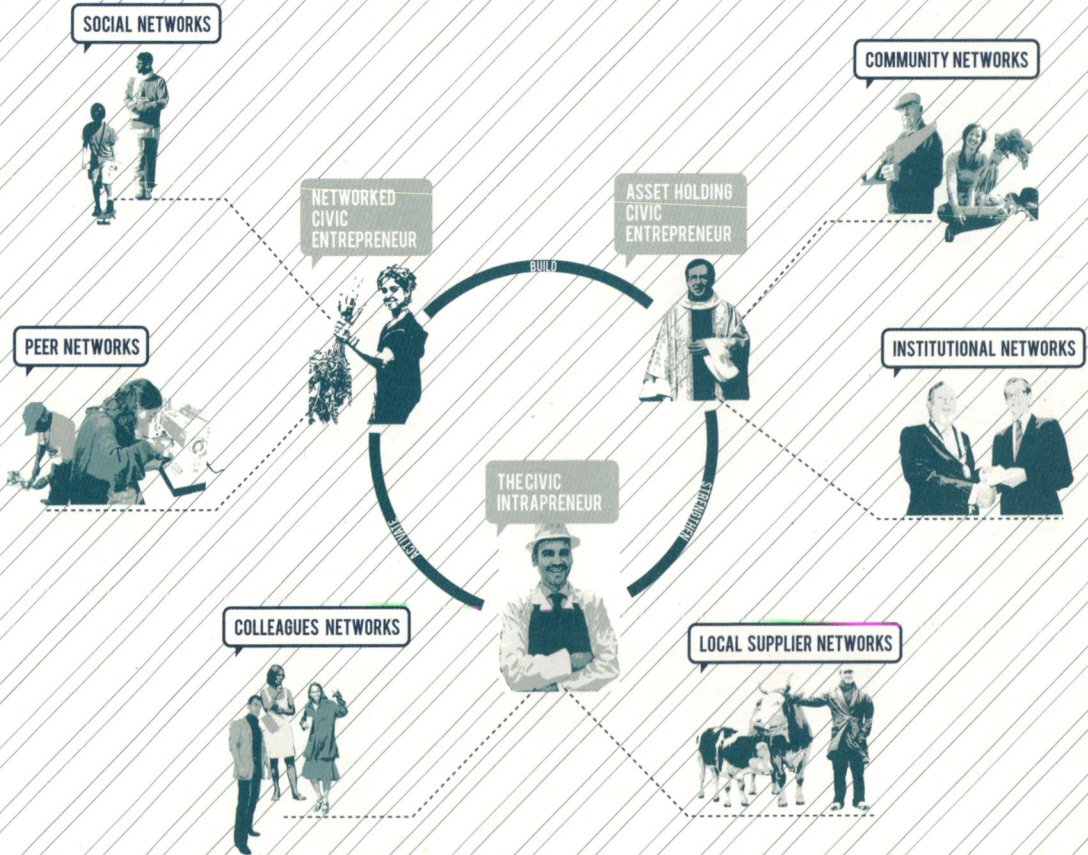

SOCIAL NETWORKS

COMMUNITY NETWORKS

NETWORKED CIVIC ENTREPRENEUR

ASSET HOLDING CIVIC ENTREPRENEUR

BUILD

PEER NETWORKS

INSTITUTIONAL NETWORKS

THE CIVIC INTRAPRENEUR

COLLEAGUES NETWORKS

LOCAL SUPPLIER NETWORKS

The initiators of the civic economy can be found in many different places and in a wide range of positions across the public, private and third sector. They can play many roles: some create opportunities through the assets they control, like the parish minister who transformed a church into a health centre and community service enterprise hub, or the founders of a theatre as open house of new ideas (**Bromley by Bow Centre, Arcola Theatre**); others through their networks, like the organiser of an intensive process to re-occupy vacant market units or the initiators of a unique private-community energy partnership (**Brixton Village, Fintry Development Trust**); and others use their embedded role within organisations to lever change, such as the hospital catering manager who helped farmers to overcome procurement hurdles (**Nottingham University Hospitals**). Irrespective of their formal role or function, these people are civic entrepreneurs. Their way of working is not dependent on their job title but rather on their passion, purpose, energy and doggedness, and how they share this with others – telling a different story of what is possible and how to achieve it. What they all have in common is their recognition that no single person or organisation can achieve change. Therefore they work through personal social networks, and use trust as a key currency to connect new ideas and achieve change.

Implications for localities:

To create fertile ground for the civic economy, the challenge is to get better at recognising civic entrepreneurship both within and outside existing organisational structures: welcoming unexpected change-makers in unpredictable places, without containing their role in any organisational silos – whether particular delivery teams, departments or innovation taskforces.

• Despite the pressure to make savings, both local authorities and other leaders in localities need to retain and attract and develop those individuals capable of providing leadership for the civic economy: those who recognise local potential or new needs, broker relations across organisational silos, and can connect emergent perspectives for change with local policies. Retaining and enhancing the capacity for what is often called 'intrapreneurship' (acting entrepreneurially within larger organisations) will be a key determinant of success. In practice, this requires people to work across narrowly defined roles in (for example) economic development, town centre management, health and care, and planning and regeneration.

• Local authorities and other leaders in localities need to build meaningful collaborations. Success can only start with the realisation that no organisation will have all the capabilities in house to act as singularly as 'the' civic entrepreneur within an area – the examples in this book show precisely the kind of fruitful partnerships that happen when large public or private sector organisations engage actively and align their purpose with change-makers from outside. As large organisations recognise they need to be platforms for the initiative of others, this opens new pathways to change and mutual learning – a deeply collaborative approach to entrepreneurship instead of mere 'consultancy'. Procurement practices and contracts for such processes need to recognise the qualities that are likely to lead to success. These include an ability to connect to emergent initiatives, to work through informal social networks and with diverse partners, to broker trust between people, and to host an agile, open-ended kind of process.

• It has been widely recognised that innovation in wider public policy and service delivery requires the empowerment of those working at the frontline. This poses a need for a culture shift towards genuine localism and distributed decision-making: it is at the local level that civic entrepreneurs and intrapreneurs, whether a school leader, a local GP or a development planner, can meaningfully engage with the opportunities and the risks involved in doing things differently – and manage such risks through genuine collaboration and mutual learning instead of avoiding them through focusing only on contractual relationships. This gives those at the frontline an important role in providing stewardship and creating space for new ventures to emerge and succeed.

B. PARTICIPATION BEYOND CONSULTATION: INVITING CITIZEN CO-PRODUCTION

WE INVITE YOU TO JOIN US ON OUR JOURNEY TO BE CO-PRODUCERS & CO-INVESTORS IN THE COMMUNITY

SHARING PASSIONS & SKILLS

CO-INVESTORS

PEER-TO-PEER SERVICES

CO-OPERATOR

STORE

CO-GOVERNANCE

CO-PRODUCER

The civic economy puts engagement with the public at its core: instead of seeing citizens as mere consumers of goods or services, it casts them in the role of co-producers: as commissioning clients for new house-building (**Tübingen User-led Housing**), providers of peer-to-peer services (**Southwark Circle**), co-developers of youth communications (**Livity**), builders of an enriched public realm (**Incredible Edible Todmorden**), or active members of a co-operative shop (**The People's Supermarket**). Co-investment from local people only works where there is strong backing for new ventures – which is why civic entrepreneurs spend a lot of time reaching out and engaging with communities, inviting in their creativity, time, energy and drive and communicating the diverse potential rewards. They know they rely on a sense of common purpose and mutual trust (often called social capital). In some cases this fertile ground already exists; in other cases, civic entrepreneurs realise that they must help build it. Underlying this is a renewed emphasis on co-production as an organisational and design principle across public services. Its role in place-making, however, is still too often underexploited, as practitioners rely on narrower or less meaningful forms of participation, such as statutory consultations that focus on the physical design of places.

Implications for localities:

To create fertile ground for the civic economy, regeneration practitioners need to learn from and work with the approaches pioneered by civic entrepreneurs and see participation in the first instance as citizen co-investment.

• Amongst the successes shown in this book are the myriad ways in which change-makers genuinely invite people to engage – embracing their strengths, sharing their purpose, showing a commitment to action, and creating plausible pathways for tangible change. Their approaches may involve the use of hyper-local websites, social media, creative events or arts-led approaches – but it is not the particular medium of such tactics that we need to learn from. What matters is grounding them in purposeful approaches that connect intelligently with local people's sense of belonging, the grain of their everyday lives, their aspirations, capabilities and attachment to place – and transcend divisions in communities

where the basis of shared trust and confidence still needs to be built. This is the only way to create genuine opportunity for the widest possible participation in the civic economy.

• The practices of the civic economy go far beyond 'consultation' or even 'co-design' – people are being invited to take part not just in decision-making but in the long-term running of spaces, shops and services. As is shown by The People's Supermarket, it is the product, not just the initial process that is participative. Civic entrepreneurs seek to create platforms where deep participation is permanently at the heart and viability of the venture. This 'we will if you will' approach helps to bond people in a relationship of mutual trust and accountability.

• Meaningful participation occurs within clear, realistic and low-threshold frameworks. Creating these frameworks is one of the core strengths of each of the examples in this book. There are many other examples of successful approaches that are already becoming more embedded in mainstream practice – the London Borough of Haringey is adopting DIY Streets, an approach developed by the charity Sustrans that lets local people take the initiative to make streets more welcoming to pedestrians, playing children and cyclists; and in many places, local third sector groups along with district and parish councillors have been at the forefront of helping local people take over local shops and post offices threatened with closure, providing the political leadership that is essential to change in localities.

C. FINANCIAL CO-INVESTMENT: DIVERSIFYING FUNDING STREAMS

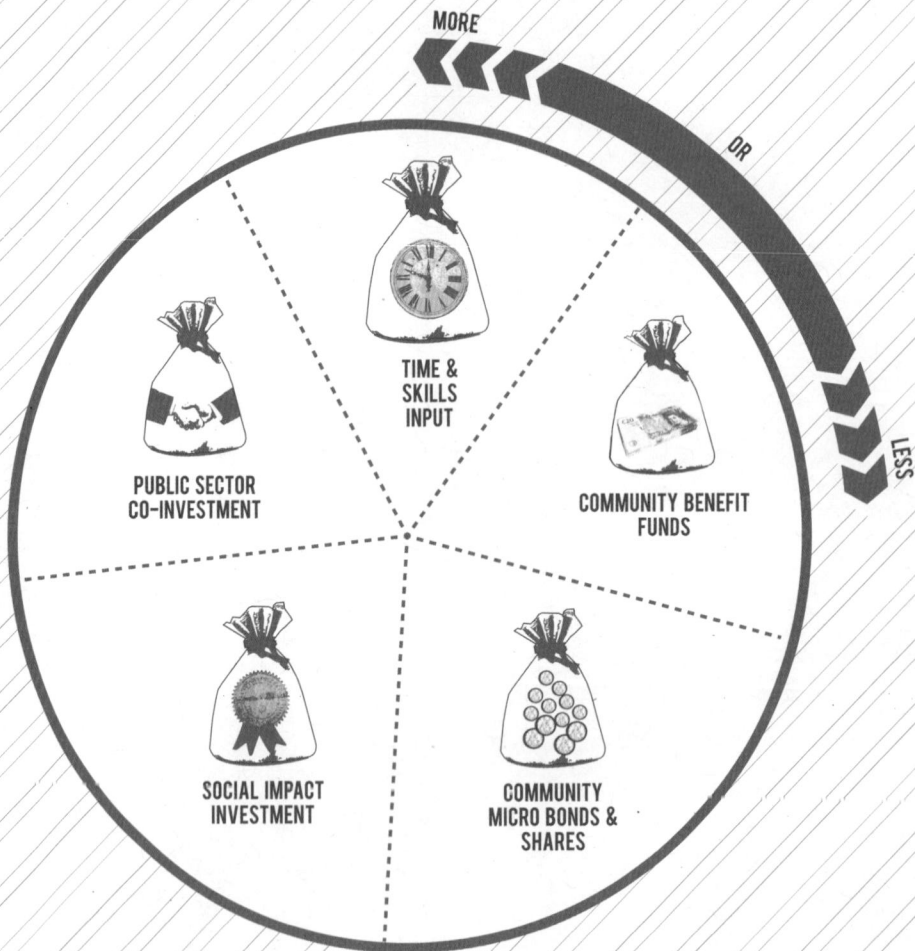

MORE

OR

LESS

TIME &
SKILLS
INPUT

PUBLIC SECTOR
CO-INVESTMENT

COMMUNITY BENEFIT
FUNDS

SOCIAL IMPACT
INVESTMENT

COMMUNITY
MICRO BONDS &
SHARES

A shift towards more diverse and mixed-mode funding strategies has already enabled projects as diverse as **Rutland Telecom**, **The George and Dragon** and **The Hub Islington**. This rapidly evolving field of co-production merits separate attention, as it encourages the public to be actively involved beyond charitable giving. Unlocking large numbers of relatively small investors enhances democratic belonging and self-reliance: it builds local communities of interest around projects with shared local value and gives them an active stake in success. Crucially, this approach goes beyond charity or the gift economy – and also, as shown by the success of **Livity**, beyond the CSR budgets of large companies. Such shifts enable a new generation of civic ventures to become financially viable, building new shared wealth and a more democratic ownership structure. Recently, more examples of innovative finance structures have revealed the wider appetite for this: the Community Shares pilot has shown how citizen investment at a micro-scale can fund local services, community buy-out of shops, and utilities; and Social Impact Bonds are one amongst many innovative finance approaches being explored to scale up social impact investment.

Implications for localities:

To create fertile ground for the civic economy, localities need to champion, test, enable and incentivise local and regional co-investment mechanisms that generate democratic belonging and co-ownership. Creating such fertile ground for financial co-investment could also have far-reaching benefits for the development process: by inviting the local community to co-invest in new projects, 'Not In My Back Yard' sentiment can be transformed into a renewed focus on shared interest.

• Localities must become more proactive in the enabling of new funding frameworks. These could be mixed-mode, recognising time and in-kind investment in parallel to monetary contributions. Practically, this could entail providing public or private match-funding for money raised through citizen co-investment schemes, as well as for volunteer time; companies viewing their CSR budgets not as stand-alone charitable giving but as an integral part of the much wider potential they have to create social returns across their investments; localities promoting and supporting projects that use community shares or bonds; and (co-)developing enabling technology such as micro-finance platforms akin to the American Kickstarter website, which raises finance for creative ventures through a highly transparent online process. As the work of Seattle's Department of Neighborhoods has shown in the US, providing leadership by widely championing successful new initiatives – and giving recognition to the entrepreneurs behind them – is integral to this approach.

• Recent experiences have also shed more light on the barriers that need to be overcome: we must build a better awareness of these opportunities and success stories amongst the public, enable good-practice sharing between budding projects in what is still an emergent sector, and find ways of providing affordable capital solutions to ventures beyond their initial seed funding and start-up capital phases. Greater sophistication within the growing social finance sector and co-development of such products with social ventures will help create resilience and access to larger amounts of capital. Developing greater community financial literacy will also be an important factor in building a better understanding of responsible risk-taking and productive asset-building. Attention also needs to be paid to how people with lower incomes can invest, such as through 'subscription shares'.

• If localities were to have a greater degree of control over local finances, this could free them to create other mechanisms to co-invest in the civic economy. In particular, local incentive schemes could vary business rates according to the civic contribution of new ventures; for example, when they build co-ownership and belonging, create local jobs, source local food, and reduce environmental impacts. Increasingly, the public sector must recognise that it needs to play a catalytic and collaborative role as one investor amongst many: the diversity of citizen and entrepreneurial co-investments – including micro-finance, time, intellectual property and reputation – should also be recognised and accounted for.

D. RE-USING EXISTING ASSETS: RECOGNISING LATENT OPPORTUNITIES

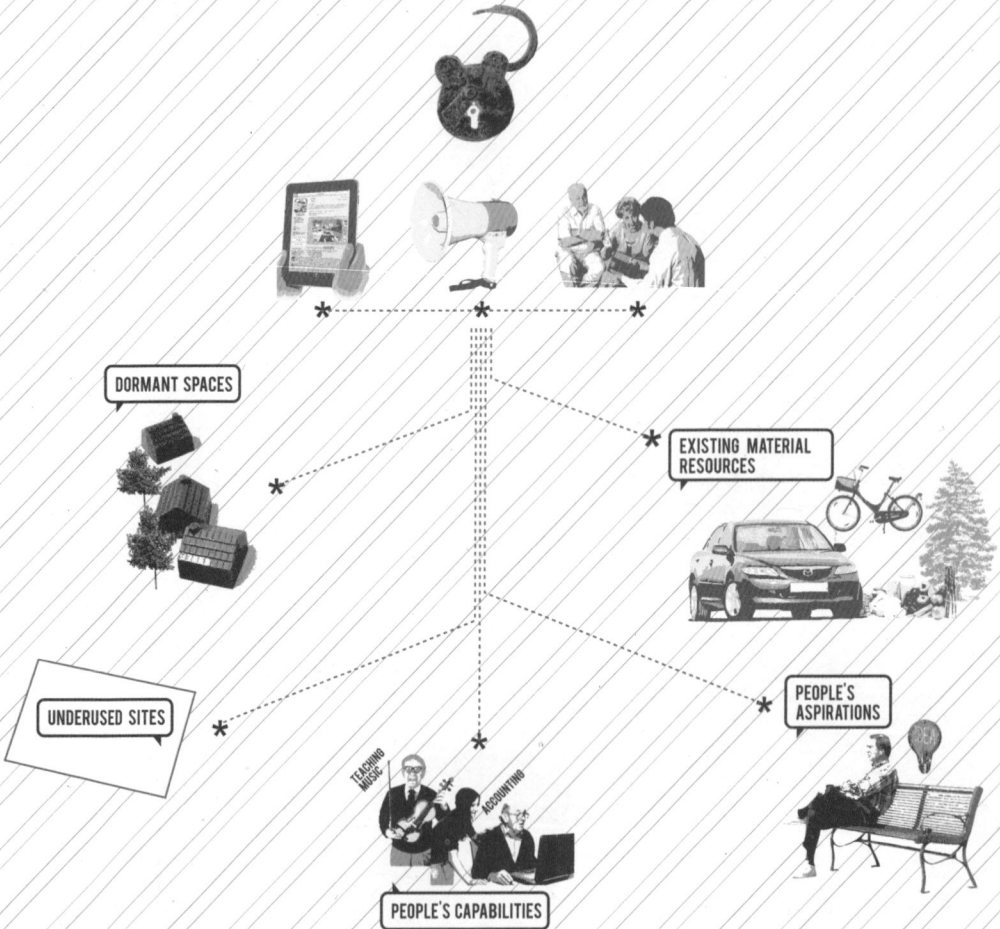

DORMANT SPACES

EXISTING MATERIAL RESOURCES

UNDERUSED SITES

PEOPLE'S ASPIRATIONS

TEACHING MUSIC

ACCOUNTING

PEOPLE'S CAPABILITIES

Most of the examples in this book are based on the recognition that places have latent assets that are underutilised or even discarded. They re-occupy buildings and spaces (**Studio Hergebruik**), make better use of abundantly available materials and resources (**Baisikeli, Neil Sutherland Architects**), create new platforms for people to share resources such as workspace or cars (**The Hub Islington; Jayride**), and devise new ways of fostering people's skills and capabilities (such as at the **Museum of East Anglian Life**). The civic economy often 'treads lightly' where it comes to the use of material resources. But fundamentally, the prosperity and future resilience of communities is not just about using less – instead, it is about recovering more, whether physical assets, human potential or local aspirations for change. In economic terms, civic ventures are often remarkably successful at matching the 'demand' of often unmet needs with the 'supply' of frequently ignored resources. The innovative potential of the civic economy therefore lies in rewiring and unleashing what we have and creating better 'software': ways of unlocking and re-combining latent potential, whether through new online technology or local collaboration. This stands in sharp contrast to a regeneration approach that has too often been synonymous with the demolition and new-build of 'hardware' made up of buildings and physical infrastructure.

Implications for localities:

Localities need to realise that fertile ground for the civic economy need not be 'built' anew or from scratch: the civic economy requires no expensive business parks or physical infrastructure. Instead, it is about rediscovering the resources that already exist, whether physical or human, and growing them. Therefore we need a shift in focus that starts with such existing assets, and values them as seedbeds for a low-cost, low-barrier-of-entry innovation economy.

• Empty buildings and land should be seen as potential assets for communities and small businesses. Brixton Village was primarily seen as a redevelopment opportunity – until Space Makers Agency showed an alternative approach. They and others like the Meanwhile Project have addressed the operational challenges of re-occupying empty buildings and sites, which many councils still struggle to make available for temporary use. However,

this should not be seen as a recession-time-only phenomenon but as part of a healthy approach to regeneration and a start-up economy: permanently maintaining a diversity of space typologies (in terms of ownership, unit size, rental levels and lease types) is crucial to make sure that local ventures can have access to affordable and flexible space and thus to the wider market at all stages in the economic cycle. Developers and landowners should be facilitated and incentivised to maintain or create these conditions both for vacant buildings and new development projects through, for example, planning gain conditions (e.g., section 106 contributions).

• Unlocking dormant assets requires a wide awareness of what is there already. Collaboratively 'mapping' the assets of places (both physical spaces and hidden talents and learning dreams) is a process that could bring policy-makers and service providers together with the wider public, creating platforms for genuine discussion about the shared aspirations for places. Such an approach was at the heart of the Brixton Village project; it has also been used elsewhere, for example, in the Leeds Love It Share It project, initiated by a group of local academics, professionals and community organisers. Such engagements should not be seen as a cost but as means to unlocking latent potential. Central to this process is the growing of people's skills and capabilities – adding further weight to points made already about participation, co-investment and empowering of frontline staff.

• Enabling more creative and participative use of vacant buildings and sites also depends on making clear what the pathway to re-occupation looks like. Allowing communities a right to use and manage local assets initially during a time-limited period could be one way to enable this. Furthermore, the rapid expansion in online sharing platforms can make available assets and resources more transparent – building on platforms such as the School of Everything (an online skills-swapping platform), Mumsnet (a peer-to-peer online advice hub), somewhere to (Livity's initiative to unlock access to spaces for youth initiative) or the growing number of local neighbourhood websites.

E. THE EXPERIENCE OF PLACE: SETTING PHYSICAL AND SOCIAL CONDITIONS

PRESENCING SHARED EXPERIENCES

PRODUCTS USED TO INSPIRE

ADAPTABLE SPACES THAT ALLOW USERS TO IMPRINT THEIR OWN STORIES

MATERIALS USED TO CONVEY ETHIC OF THE PLACE

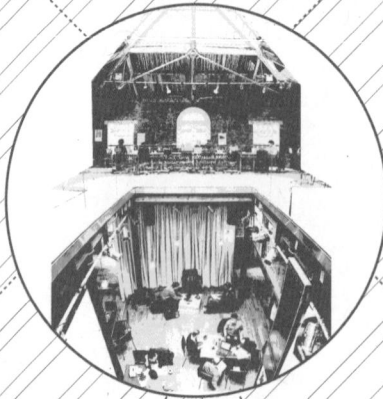

MATERIALS USED TO COMMUNICATE CO-INVESTORS

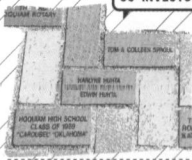

CELEBRATING PEOPLE WHO HELPED BUILD IT

In many examples in this book, civic entrepreneurs have paid particular attention to the full experience of a place: not just the physical layout, materials and aesthetics but also its social dimensions and narratives. Both are crucial to tell the story and purpose behind a venture and to invite participation. Both help create a sense of uniqueness, wonder and delight, and gently disrupt users' expectations. This is evident in the **One Love City** public space installation, which functions as a participative platform; in the ways in which mental barriers to entry are lowered in **Bromley by Bow Centre** and the **Brooklyn Superhero Supply Co.**; in the way in which the **Hørsholm Waste-to-Energy** plant is embedded in the neighbourhood instead of hidden away; or in the 'hosting' strategy of **The Hub Islington**, which creates an active place for people to meet and exchange ideas.

These projects are keenly aware of what it is that buildings and places communicate to people or enable their users to do. This is not only about the way they are designed but more fundamentally about how they are made over time through the contribution of many and with a keen eye for the details that are crucial to the story that is told. It is this approach that generates genuine local pride and belonging.

Implications for localities:

To create fertile ground for the civic economy, localities need to learn from these practices, recognise the diverse qualities and value they generate, and promote them across public, community and private development projects. Good places are never bought off the shelf, but arise in an inclusive process built on local ideas, imagination and aspiration. Short cuts and pre-packaged solutions fail if they give the message that the longer-term outcomes and processes matter less than the sheer fact of 'delivering' a building or service – an awareness that should be integral to the brief-setting of any new project.

• The examples in the case studies show that successful places cannot be mandated by planning policy alone: they need a shared awareness of how great places are made. This needs to be the subject of open and participative conversations locally. Within the public sector, planning and regeneration officers and elected repre-

sentatives play a crucial role in seeding this culture both by championing local successes and by inviting people to participate in debate. Deep community engagement and involvement is an integral and material condition in the planning process, seeding co-production not just in the design phase but also in the operationalisation and governance of places.

• Public realm strategies should be platforms that enable the contribution of community organisations and the public at large. Many participative strategies already exist; collaborative organisations such as the Bankside Open Spaces Trust in London have devised pathways for co-investment in the public realm and created significant additional tangible and intangible value.

• Even at a time of funding constraints, procurement practices and design criteria for public or community buildings and spaces need go beyond 'least cost' considerations. Good professionals are needed to lead project teams and apply their skills to reconceptualising problems and devising creative solutions through collaboration. Ingredients of success can often be achieved without significant extra cost: for example, the reception space in the Bromley by Bow Centre fosters sociability without requiring additional space or staff. What this means is that the actual day-to-day functioning of a space must be in sync with its stated purpose; if not, this impacts on an organisation's credibility and on the pride and participation of users, creating a costly waste of opportunity.

F. AN OPEN-ENDED APPROACH: FRAMEWORKS FOR EMERGENCE

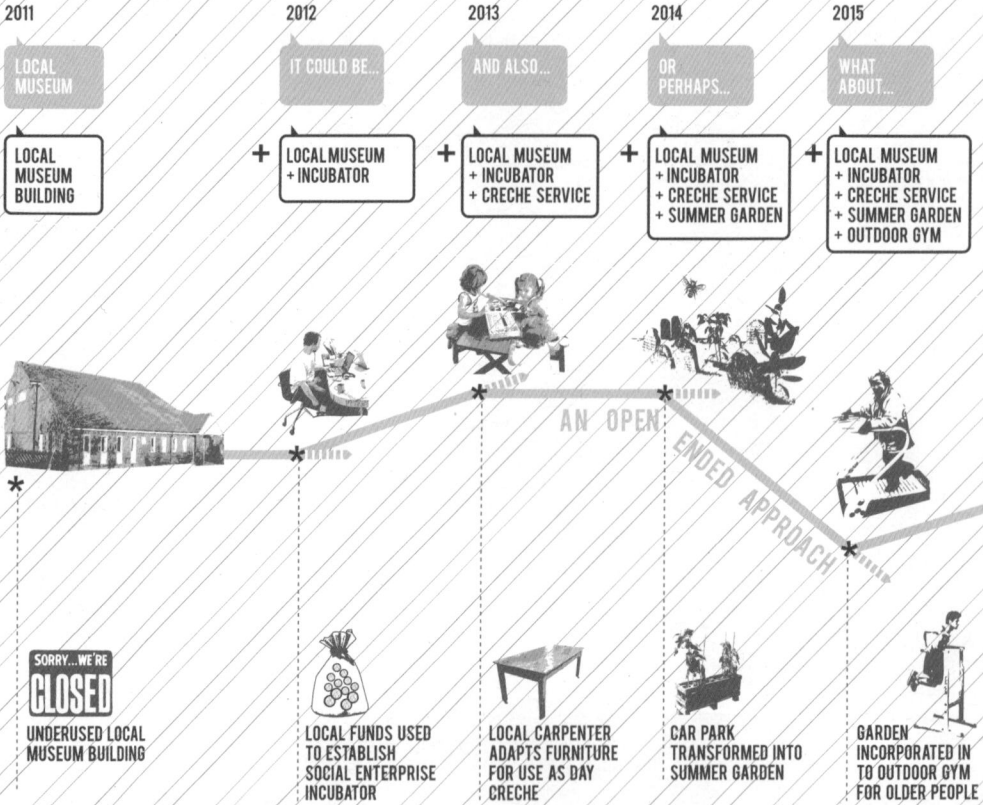

2011

LOCAL MUSEUM

LOCAL MUSEUM BUILDING

2012

IT COULD BE...

+ LOCAL MUSEUM + INCUBATOR

2013

AND ALSO...

+ LOCAL MUSEUM + INCUBATOR + CRECHE SERVICE

2014

OR PERHAPS...

+ LOCAL MUSEUM + INCUBATOR + CRECHE SERVICE + SUMMER GARDEN

2015

WHAT ABOUT...

+ LOCAL MUSEUM + INCUBATOR + CRECHE SERVICE + SUMMER GARDEN + OUTDOOR GYM

AN OPEN ENDED APPROACH

SORRY...WE'RE CLOSED

UNDERUSED LOCAL MUSEUM BUILDING

LOCAL FUNDS USED TO ESTABLISH SOCIAL ENTERPRISE INCUBATOR

LOCAL CARPENTER ADAPTS FURNITURE FOR USE AS DAY CRECHE

CAR PARK TRANSFORMED INTO SUMMER GARDEN

GARDEN INCORPORATED IN TO OUTDOOR GYM FOR OLDER PEOPLE

Few of the examples in this book came into the world as finished products. The civic economy is based on the incremental ideas and opportunity-spotting of a wide range of people over time. New ventures often start small and evolve significantly over time – such as the wealth of activities in **Bromley by Bow Centre**, the gradual opening up of the **Museum of East Anglian Life** and **Olinda Psychiatric Hospital**, or the incremental approach to building a movement in **Incredible Edible Todmorden**. The initial steps often serve to build a shared language of tangible change, building fertile ground for next endeavours – they are an investment in longer-term outcomes. The true potential of such initiatives cannot always be 'planned for' or strategically designed through prescriptive master-planning or output-based commissioning; instead, we should build the frameworks for them to emerge, starting small and iterating initiatives through wide participation. This approach – a form of 'open-source' place-making – liberates the power of individuals and communities to contribute to change, creating new markets and testing concepts that are hard to prove through precedent.

Implications for localities:

To create fertile ground for the civic economy, an incremental approach to the development and revitalisation of places is often more effective than a plan-led approach. This focuses on, for example, 'early wins', to build confidence in communities; creating space for experimental and risk-taking ventures; and appropriate local investment frameworks and tools such as meanwhile licences. More systematically, it demands informed decision-making capability at the frontline in localities and always depends on the fostering and brokering of diverse social networks and diverse opportunities for participation.

• In many places across the UK, particularly under the current market circumstances, it is more relevant to show how change can be achieved now, than to rely on long-term planning. Because of their long and formalised timescales, existing statutory planning tools such as 'Area Action Plans' or masterplans may have little relevance to enabling the civic economy in the short term (although they can play a role in ensuring conditions for the long term). Small-scale co-created public realm interventions and meanwhile uses for buildings and land show communities that change is possible and that their contributions are integral to it. Rather than resulting from statutory and strategic plans, such 'early win' projects should be seen as their precursors.

• Working from the principle of 'starting small' may require change in how investment is managed and how proposals are reviewed: micro-investments can be needed to support initial projects, along with quick decision-making capacity close to the frontline which allows for iteration and experimentation. Equally, it is important to enable a degree of open-endedness in reviewing outcomes, for example, in local authority development management (which will have to accept that the physical appearance of civic ventures may be more open-ended and dynamic than usual), and in selecting and iterating relevant metrics in reviewing the success of projects. One crucial metric, for example, is that the governance of new ventures is open and agile in the long term.

• Open-endedness also implies a series of physical conditions in the built environment to foster opportunities for civic entrepreneurs and start-up ventures. These include a fine grain of buildings and different-size floor plates; the presence of low-rent premises and spaces for informal meetings; a mix of use classes and of old and new buildings; and adaptability of open spaces. Developments should include such conditions lest they become impermeable to change or structurally favour large-scale users.

G. GENERATING CHANGE THROUGH NETWORKS: THE SCALING CHALLENGE

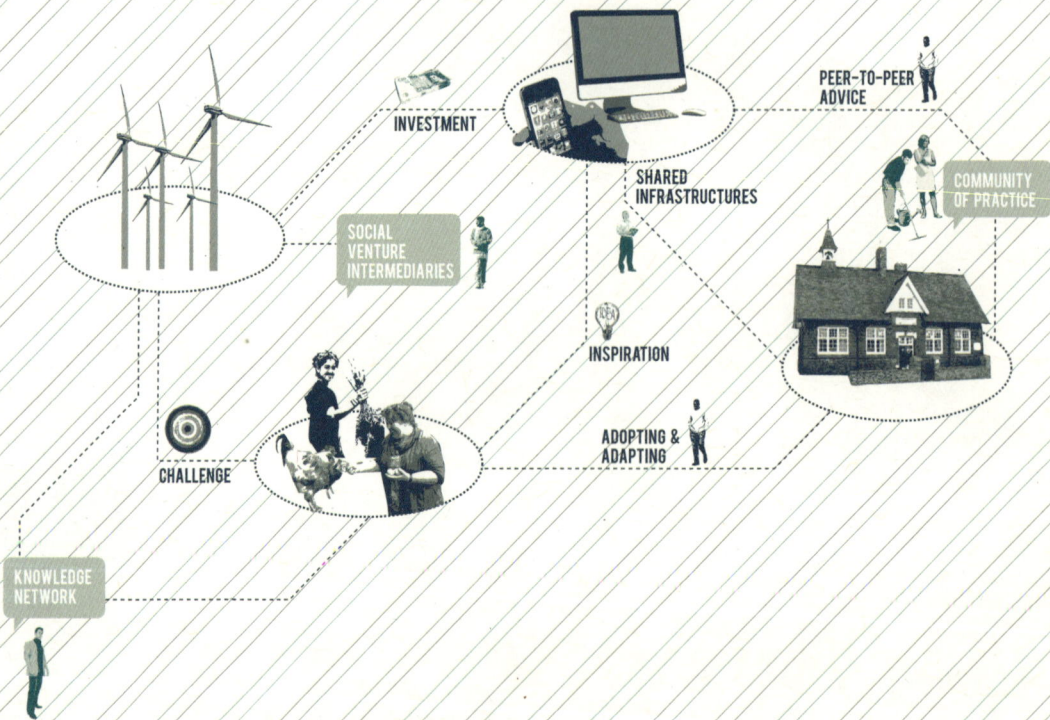

INVESTMENT

PEER-TO-PEER ADVICE

SHARED INFRASTRUCTURES

COMMUNITY OF PRACTICE

SOCIAL VENTURE INTERMEDIARIES

INSPIRATION

CHALLENGE

ADOPTING & ADAPTING

KNOWLEDGE NETWORK

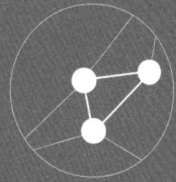

The new ventures of the civic economy may often look local; in practice, they tend to be highly networked, or at least part of a broader movement to which they look for inspiration and know-how. For example, nationwide or international communities of practice link ventures such as **Fab Lab Manchester, the Brooklyn Superhero Supply Co., Household Energy Services** and **The George and Dragon**, to ideas, a globally recognised brand, organisational infrastructure and financial resources. At the same time, civic ventures themselves have initiated new learning and peer-to-peer advice networks to enable change elsewhere, such as through **TCHO**'s Flavor Labs, or the advice that **Rutland Telecom** and the **Fintry Development Trust** give to other places. This points to different ways to scale the impact of successful ventures. In this, civic entrepreneurs tread a balance between the scope and agility offered by local embeddedness and engagement, and the fact that they are not immune to the rules of scale economies.

Implications for localities:

To create fertile ground for the civic economy, civic entrepreneurs and their collaborators in public, private and third sector institutions need to understand and value the nature of these networks – contributing as well as benefiting from them. In practice, pathways to growth and development open up when local ventures can connect to wider support networks offered by national organisations, potential funding bodies, and knowledge networks.

• New network-building frameworks are being explored already: supported 'social challenge prize' competitions such as the Big Green Challenge and the Neighbourhood Challenge provide a useful format for sourcing and supporting budding ideas, rewarding not just the winners but also helping to build the ideas of runners-up. Such collaborative competitions and knowledge exchange structures could be generated regionally and locally by working with networked civic entrepreneurs. These approaches can catalyse innovative communities of practice in ways the public sector alone cannot.

• Many of the case studies can be and have been scaled through an approach that adopts and adapts their ideas for use elsewhere. This enables growth not through sheer repetition but through creating the conditions for proliferation by the initiative of others, without a need to re-invent the wheel entirely: by combining local intelligence and purpose with shared learning, the initial concept can be translated into locally relevant conditions and opportunities. This has been called 'social franchising' – however, care needs to be taken that the entrepreneurial aspect of new ventures is maintained, avoiding a pure 'replication' approach. In the same way that the development of civic start-ups needs an open-ended approach, their further expansion requires testing and iteration of different potential approaches and models that, in the end, may change according to local circumstances.

• In some cases, new civic ventures can profit significantly from shared 'infrastructures', for example, efficiencies generated through shared supply chains or back-office functions, shared raising of finance, and the structured sharing of know-how. There will be an important role for the 'social venture intermediaries' that facilitate such shared infrastructures and learning networks: whether through physically shared spaces or web-based channels, the challenge is to seed, maintain and grow real communities of practice. As part of this, we need to develop better strategies to work with and learn from new civic enterprises that are struggling.

• Southwark Circle's peer-to-peer service provision and The Hub Islington's workspace and business support model are both examples of organisations that seek to expand in order to reach long-term sustainability. Local change-makers and entrepreneurs could tap into this by developing local initiatives that adopt and adapt their original ideas. Eventually this could lead to further proactive involvement of civic entrepreneurs and social venture intermediaries in co-developing more responsive financial infrastructures and regulatory arrangements that enable greater permeability of, for example, public sector procurement or self-provision of utilities to smaller providers.

H. RECOGNISING WHERE VALUE LIES : THE METRICS OF CHANGE

LONG TERM
ECONOMIC
RETURNS

ENVIROMENTAL
RETURNS

SOCIAL & WELL
BEING
RETURNS

DIVERSITY OF
LOCAL
PROVIDERS

ENVIRONMENTAL
COSTS

SOCIAL & WELL BEING
COSTS

ECONOMIC SHORT
TERMISM

DOMINANT
MONOPOLIES

Some of the value created by the civic economy can be measured – such as the new jobs and training delivered by the **Museum of East Anglian Life**, the products developed in **Fab Lab Manchester**, or the carbon and money saved by the **Hørsholm Waste-to-Energy** plant. Other outcomes are less clear-cut: the value generated by a more diverse experience on high streets, by the personal approach of protagonists, by the many ways in which local people are invited to participate and the confidence and capabilities this gives them. Both types of value are real – and both need to be recognised and better represented in decision-making and commissioning processes, along with the relevant metrics to measure them. A healthy competition regime is necessary for economic flourishing but the market in many cases favours established corporate providers, causing hurdles for ventures such as **Rutland Telecom**. Ultimately, it is this institutional shift, creating a better interface between the 'micro' and the 'massive', that is required to grow the civic economy.

Implications for localities:

To create fertile ground for the civic economy, localities need to recognise that if they seek genuine community resilience, well-being and belonging, this should affect the way things are done across their operations. This implies the need for different procurement and commissioning methods and performance metrics. These are integral to the culture change required to foster the civic economy.

• The increasing attention at national level to a broader range of outcomes – including well-being indicators – is welcome, particularly if it creates opportunities to question how our economy is structured, owned and co-produced. Local people must drive the debate about what local well-being means, how it is related to the economies of places, and how this affects the metrics by which we measure progress. In the Scottish town of Neilston, for example, such debates led to the collaborative creation of a town charter and the development of new civic ventures. Such processes could be part of the formal planning system but could also take place more informally, through dedicated online community platforms and 'open government' web platforms that enable debate about local opportunities, assets, problems and risks.

• A better understanding of how new approaches to social impact investment can inform decision-making and unlock finance is required so that local authorities and other local actors can use this tool more proactively. Innovative finance such as social impact investment and other mechanisms that encourage positive social or environmental impact beyond financial return could unlock private capital for shared purposes and inform debates about outcome measurement. At the same time we also need to take into account the open-ended nature of many successful civic ventures – led by the deep return on investment of people's passion, creativity and drive, which cannot always be captured by quantitative metrics.

• In order to create a level playing field for civic entrepreneurs, it is necessary to recognise and incentivise some of the core characteristics and values of the civic economy over pure 'best price' and 'risk minimisation'. This requires, on the one hand, civic entrepreneurs to be increasingly sophisticated in demonstrating the diversity of value they create – but it also takes public sector leadership. Public sector procurement policies as well as regulatory enforcement in sectors such as telecoms and energy are integral to this. They should be more actively aware of the role they can play to foster the civic economy – and the cost of ignoring it. Practical examples include the stipulation of meanwhile strategies and affordable workspace provisions as part of planning and development proposals; tax incentives for civic ventures; provisions for space to be set aside for independent operators in retail and office developments; setting aside a proportion of the services or works for innovative or alternative providers such as new mutuals; 'local' (food/labour/material) clauses for public sector procurement, through better accounting for transport miles or carbon impact; preferencing of small-scale and user-driven developer types in housing developments; or the preferential treatment of communities over corporate parties in asset transfer processes.

IN ORDER TO CREATE THE FERTILE
GROUND FOR THE CIVIC ECONOMY,
WE MUST START TO RE-IMAGINE AND
RE-BUILD IN THE BROADEST SENSE
THE 'INSTITUTIONAL ECONOMICS'
OF PLACE.

BUILDING A CIVIC ECONOMY FUTURE

Amongst the diverse lessons presented in this chapter, one shared recommendation stands out: building fertile ground for the civic economy requires a change in practice across all sectors of society. Providing fertile ground for civic entrepreneurs is about embedding a different way of thinking and doing, not about quick fix solutions, extensive new legislation or huge capital investment programmes such as in business parks or other physical infrastructure. A positive, optimistic and collaborative culture is the most important platform on which the civic economy can emerge and grow.

Already, within the current policy context, people have found ways to overcome constraints in the status quo, in order to generate collaborations between organisations, foster experiments and broker deals that enable promising ideas. Such examples of civic entrepreneurship or intrapreneurship show that sometimes it is the perception rather than the reality of something actually being impossible that impedes innovation. Nor is this an issue of the public sector 'getting out of the way': more than anything the civic economy requires a shift in mindset that welcomes and encourages the leadership and initiative of a wide range of people both within and outside established organisations.

We hope that the 25 ventures that we have described will inspire you, but at the same time it is clear that these are not templates to cut out and replicate. Creating a civic economy is not about scaling any one particular approach but creating a broader movement that unleashes people to create new shared solutions within a collaborative and supportive environment. This is not a mere dream: our case studies show that where such relations have been built at a local level, responsibility for change can also be shared – with unexpected partners from a wide range of backgrounds.

At the same time we need to recognise that the emerging civic economy, in all its richness, is still fragile, and we cannot predict how the civic ventures in this book will fare. In particular, we have to acknowledge the very real pressures on people's lives, whether in economic terms or because of the many demands on their time, commitment and energy. That is why the most successful projects and approaches are those that work with the grain of daily lives and respond to local capabilities, needs and opportunities. In doing so, there is an evident tension between valuing the civic economy and the pressure to achieve lowest cost in all situations – investment of creativity, time and intelligence is required to unlock the latent resources of people and places. However, wasting these resources is simply not something we can afford. The UK needs the civic economy to flourish and grow, and this is the moment to create the fertile ground for that to happen.

PHOTOGRAPHS

	Case studies	Cover image
#01	Arcola Theatre	Arcola Theatre
#02	Baisikeli	Leif Tuxen
#03	Brixton Village	Andy Broomfield
#04	Bromley by Bow Centre	Wyatt MacLaren Architects LLP
#05	Brooklyn Superhero Supply Co.	00:/
#06	Fab Lab Manchester	Fab Lab Manchester
#07	Fintry Development Trust	Pete Skabara
#08	The George and Dragon	The George and Dragon
#09	Household Energy Services	00:/
#10	The Hub Islington	Left & bottom left : Christian de Sousa dancingeye.net, Others : 00:/
#11	Hørsholm Waste-to-Energy	Dennis Lehmann
#12	Incredible Edible Todmorden	Incredible Edible Todmorden
#13	Jayride	00:/
#14	Livity	Teri Pengilley
#15	Museum of East Anglian Life	Museum of East Anglian Life
#16	Neil Sutherland Architects	Neil Sutherland Architects
#17	Nottingham University Hospitals	00:/
#18	Olinda Psychiatric Hospital	La Fabbrica di Olinda
#19	One Love City	Peter Skjalm for Bureau Detours
#20	The People's Supermarket	00:/
#21	Rutland Telecom	Rutland Telecom
#22	Southwark Circle	Southwark Circle
#23	Studio Hergebruik	Lotte Stekelenburg
#24	TCHO	TCHO
#25	Tübingen User-led Housing	Courtesy of CABE. By Christian Junge

Example left	Example centre	Example right
Watershed	junk4funk	Andrés Monroy-Hernández
Maya Riser-Kositsky	Daniel Morgan for Umlautcollective.com	First Step Trust
FLUID	Meanwhile Space	Somewhere
Deutsch lernen in Glossop	Cabinet Office	The Hill in Abergavenny
Alistair Hall	Hackney Pirates	Fighting Words
Rain Ashford	TechShop	MadLabUK
Energy4All Limited	Jørgen Schytte	Ecotricity Group Ltd
Yarpole Community Shop	Alex Parke	Topsham Ales
Stephen Shepherd	ONZO	Summerfield Eco Village
OpenSpace	Hub Culture	Centre for Social Innovation
SITA Isle of Man	Ejdzej & Iric	Torrs Hydro Ltd
Middlesbrough Town Meal	prinzessinnengarten	Nick Saltmarsh
RelayRides	Airbnb	NeighborGoods
Knowle West Media Centre	JISC infoNet	10thousandgirl
Laura Mtungwazi	Brian Pettinger	Palais de Tokyo
Scrap Pile	The Delabole Slate Company Ltd	LHOON
Raploch URC Limited	Forum for the Future	Telefonica O2 UK Ltd
Solihull Mind	Arts for Recovery in the Community	Favela Adventures
00:/	Michel Loiselle	Andreas Lang
Estelle Brown	Sugar Pond	Slaithwaite Co-operative Limited
The Phone Co-op	ganatronic	Arjan Tupan
Lewis Wright	School of Everything	Timber Wharf Time Bank
gasometri	Worn Again	Anna L Conti
Osted Mejeri	Midshires Clothing Factory	Whomadeyourpants?
Architype	Stephen Hill	Marije van den Berg

The 00:/ project team

Timothy Ahrensbach was a researcher and co-author of this publication. Having joined 00:/ in 2010, he works on innovation and creativity in urban change and focuses specifically on the potential for inter-urban learning across the hemispheres.

Joost Beunderman was a researcher and co-author of this book. His work at 00:/ straddles research and strategy from the city level to the intricate social dynamics of spaces for young people – and much in between.

Alice Fung was lead designer of the Compendium. She is a co-founder of 00:/ and Hub Make Lab. She works on strategic design projects that focus on the development of social institutions and places. She was the lead designer on The Hub King's Cross and provides design and innovation support for the Hub network.

Indy Johar was producer and co-author of this piece. He is an architect and co-founding director of 00:/, where his current work is focused on designing the new economics of place and re-building 21st Century institutions. Indy is a Director of the global Hub Association and co-founder of Hub Make Lab. He is an associate of the think-tank Demos and a fellow of Respublica.

Joni Steiner was the illustrator-in-chief of this production. A longtime member of 00:/, he was project architect on the Bristol Urban Beach, a collaboration of 00:/ with think tank Demos in the summer of 2007 and is lead architect on the refurbishment of the Winch youth community centre in north London.

Commissioning team

Laura Bunt co-commissioned this book for NESTA, and has helped to guide and reflect on its content throughout. At NESTA, Laura's work focuses on social innovation and innovation in public services. She brings this perspective to the book, exploring how these vibrant social ventures have been developed, grown and spread.

Rachel Fisher co-commissioned this book on behalf of CABE, where she was a Senior public affairs advisor. Now at the Design Council CABE she is head of policy and programmes. She's interested in the interaction between places and innovation, and particularly in how this can help drive regeneration in towns and cities.

Our collaborators

Copy-editor
Anne-Marie Conway

Design production
Mimmo Cangiano Belcuore

Printing
Calverts, a social enterprise and workers' co-operative

Acknowledgements

The 00:/ team would like to thank all those people who have contributed to this book at various stages. Rohan Silva at Number 10 Downing Street played a crucial role in inspiring this book. We would also like to acknowledge everyone involved with the 25 case studies who helped us put the stories together, generously giving their time, knowledge and feedback. Of course our colleagues at various stages have been involved with the project in so many different ways – this book is really a co-production of all of 00:/. Another invaluable collaborator was Dan Hill; the conclusion in particular benefited greatly from his reflections and input. We also had great conversations with many different people over the course of the project – we would like to mention Clive Dutton at Newham Council and Cllr Liam Maxwell of the Royal Borough of Windsor and Maidenhead in particular, as well as Anna Warrington (Forum for the Future), Ian Brenkley (RenewablesUK) and Tommaso Vitale (Sciences Po Paris) for additional information on case studies; Myfanwy Taylor (LSE Cities Research) and Hannah Leask (Brent Council) for feedback on the near-final document; and the participants at a roundtable discussion at NESTA on 5 April 2011. Priceless also was the input of Jane Harrison (Brent Council) who helped us greatly with the research in the early days, and who generously also gave us feedback later on. Elliot Erwin helpfully gave us his perspective on the book design as an intern in January 2011, and Sarah Buchan (UCL) provided vital support in the last stages of production. Siôn Whellens, Anne-Marie Conway and Mimmo Cangiano Belcuore proved themselves true collaborators in the printing, copy-editing and design production process respectively; Liam Murphy gave us crucial support in the final proofreading stage. Finally, we are deeply thankful to our partners at CABE and NESTA – in particular Rachel Fisher, Tom Bolton and Laura Bunt – for their support, insights, patience and for being critical friends throughout. As always, all errors and omissions remain our own.